Ulysses Travel Guide

EL SALVADOR

Eric Hamovitch

Ulysses Travel Publications

Series Director Claude Morneau	*English Editor* Jennifer McMorran	*Cartography* André Duchesne
Project Coordinator Pascale Couture	*Layout* Carol Wood Pierre Daveluy	*Graphic Design* Jean-François Bienvenue
Research and Composition Eric Hamovitch	*Collaboration* Daniel Desjardins	*Photography* Karl Kunmels (Superstock)

Special thanks : René Kirouac and Lise Beauchamp (Royal Vacances); Nanouska (*Instituto Salvadoreño de Turismo*).

Distributors

CANADA :
Ulysses Books & Maps
4176 Saint-Denis
Montréal, Québec
H2W 2M5
☎ (514) 843-9882, ext. 2232
Fax : 514-843-9448

GERMANY :
Brettschneider Fernreisebedarf GmbH
D-8011 Poing bei München
Hauptstr. 5
☎ 08121-71436
Fax : 08121-71419

ITALY
Edizioni Del Riccio
50143 Firenze -
Via di Soffiano, 164/A
☎ (055) 716350
Fax :(055) 713333

NETHERLANDS and FLANDERS :
Nilsson & Lamm
Pampuslaan 212-214
Postbus 195
1380 AD Weesp (NL)
☎ 02940-65044
Fax : 02940-15054

U.S.A. :
Seven Hills Book Distributors
49 Central Avenue
Cincinnati, Ohio, 45202
☎ 1-800-545-2005
Fax : (513) 381-0753

SPAIN
Altaïr
Balmes 69
E-08007 Barcelona
☎ (34-3) 323-3062
Fax : (34-3) 451-2559

SWITZERLAND :
OLF S.A.
PO BOX 1061
CH-1701 Fribourg
☎ 41 37 83 51 11
Fax : 41 37 26 63 60

Other countries, contact Ulysses Books & Maps (Montréal), Fax : (514) 843-9448

Canadian Cataloguing in Publication Data

Hamovitch, Eric

    El Salvador

    (Ulysses travel guides)
    Includes index.
    Issued also in French under title : El Salvador.

ISBN 2-921444-89-5

1. El Salvador - Guidebooks. I. Title. II. Series.

F1483.5.H25   1994   917.28404'53   C94-941539-1

© November 1994, Ulysses Travel Publications
All rights reserved
ISBN 2-921444-89-5

*Edificada con las manos del hombre,
la casa guarda al hombre y a sus manos
para que al nacer al día salga al mundo
llevando intacta la llama de la creación.*

—Salvadoran poet Roque Dalton

Edified with human hands,
the house shelters the human and his hands
so that when the day is born the world may emerge
bringing intact the flame of creation.

TABLE OF CONTENTS

A PORTRAIT OF EL SALVADOR ..	9
Geography	10
Flora and Fauna	12
History	13
Politics	17
Economy	19
Society and Culture	20
Arts and Leisure	21
PRACTICAL INFORMATION	23
Entrance Formalities	23
Customs	24
Embassies and Consulates ..	25
Tourist Information	28
Entering the Country	29
Insurance	31
Health	31
Climate	33
Packing	33
Safety and Security	34
Transportation	35
Money and Banking	39
Language	42
Mail and Telecommunications	43
Accommodation	44
Restaurants	45
Entertainment	47
Shopping	48
Press and Broadcasting	48
Miscellaneous	49
OUTDOOR ACTIVITIES	51
Beaches and Swimming ...	51
Surfing	52
Boating	52
Nature Reserves	52
Hiking	52
Bicycling	52
Tennis and Golf	53
SAN SALVADOR	55
Finding Your Way Around ..	57
Practical Information	60
Exploring	62
Parks and Beaches	67
Outdoor Activities	68
Accommodation	68
Restaurants	72
Entertainment	76
Shopping	78
CENTRAL EL SALVADOR	81
Finding Your Way Around ..	82
Exploring	84
Parks and Beaches	89
Outdoor Activities	92
Accommodation	93
Restaurants	95
Entertainment	96
Shopping	97
WESTERN EL SALVADOR	99
Finding Your Way Around ..	100
Exploring	102
Parks and Beaches	109
Outdoor Activities	111
Accommodation	112
Restaurants	115
Entertainment	116
Shopping	117
EASTERN EL SALVADOR	119
Finding Your Way Around ..	120
Exploring	123
Parks and Beaches	129
Outdoor Activities	131
Accommodation	131
Restaurants	134
Entertainment	136
Shopping	136
GLOSSARY	137

LIST OF MAPS

Central El Salvador	p 85
Eastern El Salvador	p 125
El Salvador and its Departments	p 11
San Salvador and Environs	p 63
San Salvador Centre and West	p 65
Western El Salvador	p 103
Where is El Salvador	p 7

Help make Ulysses Travel Guides even better!

The information contained in this guide was correct at press time. However, mistakes can slip in, omissions are always possible, places can disappear, etc. We value your comments, corrections and suggestions, as they allow us to keep each guide up to date.

The best contributions will be rewarded with a free book from Ulysses Travel Publications. All you have to do is write us at the following address and indicate which title you would be interested in receiving (see the list at the end).

Ulysses Travel Publications
4176 - rue Saint-Denis
Montréal, Québec
Canada H2W 2M5

TABLE OF SYMBOLS

☎	Telephone number
⇄	Fax number
≡	Air conditioning
⊗	Ceiling fan
⊗	Table fan
≈	Pool
ℜ	Restaurant
⊛	Whirlpool
ℝ	Refrigerator
ℂ	Kitchenette
tv	Colour television
MC	Mastercard accepted
VI	Visa accepted
AE	American Express accepted
DC	Diner's Club accepted

ATTRACTION CLASSIFICATION

★	Interesting
★★	Worth a visit
★★★	Not to be missed

HOTEL CLASSIFICATION

Accomodation prices are for double occupancy and include taxes, unless otherwise indicated.

RESTAURANT CLASSIFICATION

Restaurant prices are for a meal for one person, not including taxes and drinks, unless otherwise indicated.

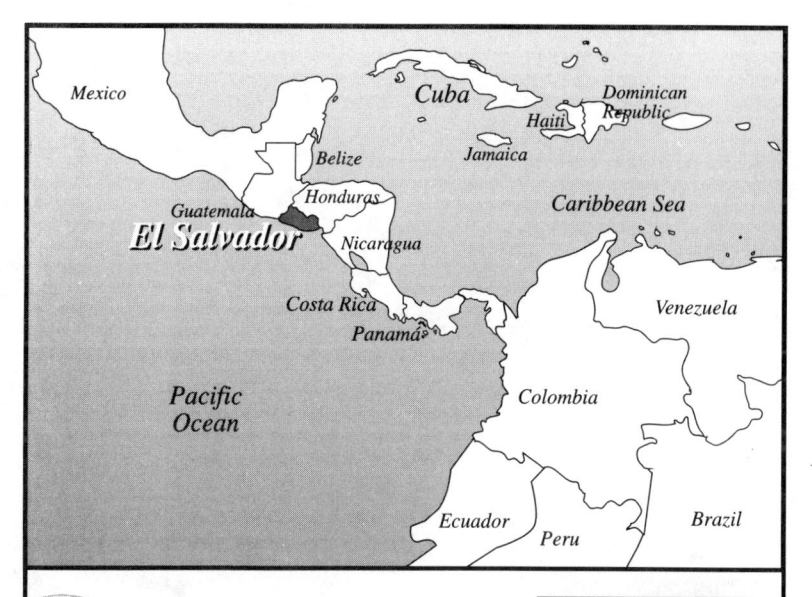

Where is El Salvador

El Salvador
Capital: San Salvador
Language: Spanish
Population: 6,000,000
Currency: Colón
Area: 21,041 km²

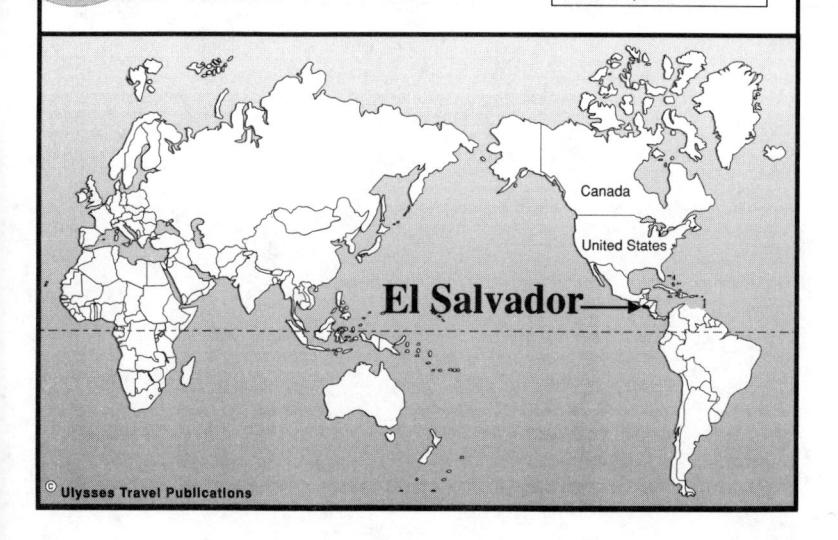

© Ulysses Travel Publications

Economy
Geography
History
Politics
Society

A PORTRAIT OF EL SALVADOR

Tourism in El Salvador? Not so long ago the very idea seemed preposterous. Here was a country wracked by civil war in the 1980s, when it became better known for death squads than for sandy beaches or clear mountain lakes, more famous for abusive military officers than for scenic volcanoes or gorgeous coffee domains, more renowned for social injustice than for colonial architecture or fine handicrafts.

Times have since changed. A peace treaty signed under United Nations auspices ended the fighting early in 1992, and elections in 1994 led to former guerrilla combatants taking seats in the legislative assembly alongside their former enemies. Areas of the country where travel used to be risky because of military activity have reopened to normal traffic flows.

It has become possible to think of El Salvador as a country rather than as a war. The arrival of peace does not mean that all of El Salvador's problems have suddenly ended or that the country is about to burst overwhelmingly upon the world tourism scene. It does mean that discerning travellers can venture freely and discover the country's many pleasures and attractions, unhindered for the time being by large crowds of tourists.

People in the travel industry sometimes make comparisons with neighbouring countries and point to what El Salvador does not have. Here are a few of the things it does have. It has lush mountain areas with beautiful hillsides planted in zigzag patterns of coffee and shade trees. It has dramatic volcanoes which can be climbed by the adventurous or appreciated from a distance. It has traditional towns with cobbled streets, red-tile roofs and a special timeless quality. It has skilled artisans who produce an array of colourful and distinctive handicrafts that are found nowhere else. It has crashing waves and a choice of black or white sand beaches along its broad Pacific coast, and it has peaceful lakes high in the hills. It has estuaries and nature reserves teeming with birdlife, several small archeological sites, countless colonial churches, and a new museum in a remote mountain town celebrating El Salvador's revolutionary movement. Most of all, it has millions of people who are hard-working and straightforward but who also display a genuine warmth and charm.

This is not to say that everything is hunky-dory. Grinding poverty remains a fact of daily life for large numbers of El Salvador's people, and the huge disparities in wealth that have blemished Salvadoran society for centuries seem unlikely to vanish any time soon. Nearly six million people are squeezed onto this small territory. To keep everyone provided for, the development of manufacturing and services has to pick up where agriculture has left off.

The tourism industry is busy reinventing itself after a long hiatus. The country's new international airport was built near the Pacific coast in the late 1970s and began operations in January 1980, just in time for the outbreak of civil war. Tourism development now has to make up for lost time. The number of good hotels remains limited, and getting around can be slow and uncomfortable. The energy and enterprise of El Salvador's people will correct this in the years to come. Tourism is no substitute for other forms of economic development, but it can generate thousands of jobs and provide new opportunities alongside other sectors of the economy.

Charter flights have begun to arrive, carrying winter-weary vacationers to Pacific coast beaches. Some of these travellers will happily find a stretch of idyllic beach to call their own, while others will take to the backroads in search of adventure climbing volcanoes, visiting villages where handicrafts are produced, or learning how coffee is grown. They will be preceded by business people coming to explore opportunities for trade and investment in a country with a strong work ethic and an interesting geographic position.

Again, El Salvador is not the most obvious place to choose for a vacation, but obvious places are rarely the most interesting. Tourism is still young enough that those who do go in the next little while can enjoy a special experience and claim legitimately to be pioneers.

Geography

El Salvador, literally "The Saviour," is the smallest, most densely populated country in the Americas. With an area of 21,041 square kilometres (8,115 square miles), it is about the size of Massachusetts and little more than half the size of the Netherlands. Its population was estimated in 1994 at close to six million, with just under half living in urban areas. The country is partly covered by mountains, which gives some idea of population densities in the more arable rural areas.

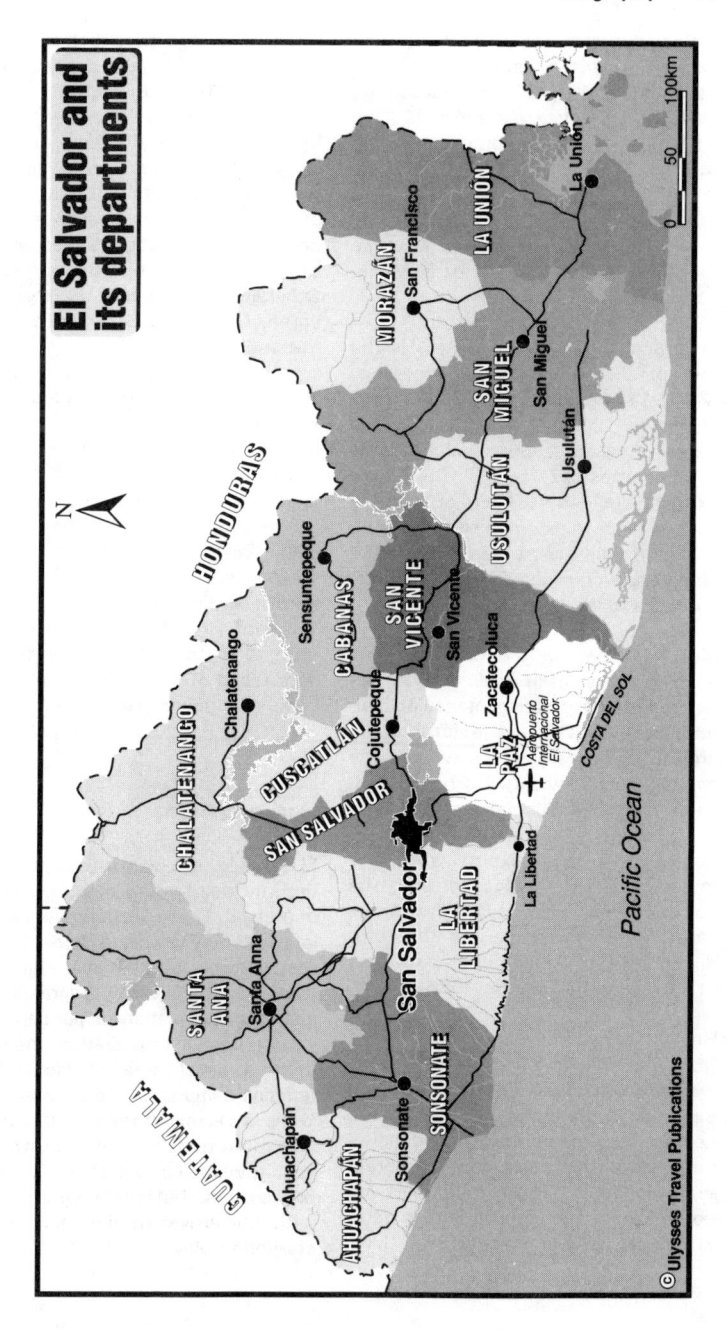

Geography 11

A Portrait of El Salvador

El Salvador is the only country on the Central American isthmus with no Caribbean coast. Its Pacific coastline, however, stretches an ample 320 km (199 mi) and includes some fine surfing beaches. El Salvador borders Guatemala to the west, Honduras to the north and east, and the Pacific Ocean to the south. Nicaragua lies a short distance southeast across the Gulf of Fonseca, but there is no land border.

A particular geographic feature is the two parallel rows of volcanoes, of which 14 are more than 900 metres (2,953 ft) high. The highest is the Santa Ana volcano, which soars 2,365 metres (7,759 ft). Most are extinct, but others have erupted at various times in recorded history. Three of them, Santa Ana, Izalco and San Miguel, are considered to be "resting" but not extinct.

Rich soils around the base of each volcano made these areas very attractive to farmers, creating intense agricultural activity. This led in turn to the growth of the larger towns. Even the capital, San Salvador, lies near a volcano. Volcanic soils are well suited to the production of coffee, which is El Salvador's biggest export crop. The tectonic instability which created the volcanoes has also caused numerous earthquakes, including one that produced serious damage and heavy loss of life in San Salvador in 1986.

Heavily farmed lowlands stretch inward from the Pacific coast, and another area of lowlands lies north of the volcano belt in the broad valley of the Río Lempa. The area of most rugged mountains lies further north near the border with Honduras. These mountains are not volcanic. The highest peak is Cerro El Pital, at 2,730 metres (8,957 ft).

The country has more than 300 rivers, none of them navigable over significant distances. The Río Lempa is the most important, and its flow is interrupted by four hydroelectric dams. It rises in Guatemala and crosses a corner of Honduras along its 350-km (217 mi) course, which takes it eastward across northern El Salvador and then south to the Pacific near the Costa del Sol. Other important rivers are the Goascorán, Grande de San Miguel, Torol, Paz and Jiboa.

There are several large mountain lakes and artificial reservoirs. Lago de Ilopango covers 72 km^2 (28 mi^2) and reaches a depth of 248 metres (814 ft), while Lago de Coatepeque covers 26 km^2 (10 mi^2) and is 120 metres (385 ft) deep. Both fill the craters of extinct volcanoes. Lago de Suchitlán, also known as Embalse Cerrón Grande, is 135 km^2 (52 mi^2) in area and 80 metres (262 ft) deep. It was created as a result of the damming of the Río Lempa for power generation.

Flora and Fauna

El Salvador has varied tropical vegetation, including more than 200 species of orchids. These are in flower between late February and late April. Most of the natural forest cover has been destroyed to allow for agriculture or pasturage. Less than six per cent of the country remains forested. In the mountains a small area of cloud forest remains damp and verdant year round, while in the rest of the country, vegetation often turns yellow or brown each year toward the end of the six-month dry season, but the verdure returns with the arrival of the rains, usually starting in May.

The higher mountain areas have temperate grasslands and remnants of the original pine and oak forests. The central plains and valleys have some small deciduous trees, bushes and subtropical grasslands, while the coastal plains and the lower slopes of the southern mountains are covered by some savanna and deciduous forest. Tree species include balsam, cedar, mahogany, laurel, nispero, madrecadao and maquilishuat, some of these highly prized by furniture makers. In the southern zone coconut palms are common. Other fruit-bearing trees include tamarind, mango, and various types of melon.

A series of estuaries and lagoons along the Pacific coast, as well as a few marshy areas inland, attract many species of birds. These include wild duck, white heron, royal heron, urraca (noted for its blue breast and grey head) and blue jay. There are also several species of turtle and crocodile. Inland, Cerro Verde national park is home to more than 120 bird species, including 17 species of hummingbirds. The Montecristo nature reserve, near the Guatemalan and Honduran borders, is one of very few breeding grounds for the quetzal, that almost mythical creature with its brilliant plumage and long tail. Toucans can also be spotted in some areas.

Heavy deforestation has destroyed the natural habitats of certain animal species such as jaguars and crested eagles, and the creation of nature reserves has done little to halt their disappearance, although efforts are now being stepped up. Among wild animals, there are scarcely any large mammals left in El Salvador, although in some northern areas there are a few deer and peccaries, a type of wild hog.

History

■ Amerindians and Spanish: 200 B.C.-1800

Olmec Indians from eastern Mexico settled in El Salvador at least 4,000 years ago, though some evidence suggests they may have arrived much earlier than that. Archeological remains are more abundant from the classic Maya period, between the third and ninth centuries A.D. Various groups settled in El Salvador at that time, including the Lenca, who lived in what is now eastern El Salvador. Central and western parts of the country were occupied by Pipil Indians, who migrated from Mexico in the 11th century and established a realm they called Cuscatlán. They formed part of the Nahua group and were related to the Aztecs, who later built an empire in central Mexico. Until the Spanish arrived, the Pipil kept close ties with neighbouring societies, including the Maya. Their few direct descendants speak a language resembling Nahuatl, still widely used today in parts of Mexico. Many place names in El Salvador bear witness to their long presence.

When the Spanish came, they found a sparsely populated country with little of the mineral wealth they were seeking. The military conquest of the Pipil was led by the notoriously cruel Pedro de Alvarado, an aide to Hernán Cortés, conqueror of the Aztecs in Mexico. Alvarado failed on his first attempt in 1524, when he crossed into El Salvador from Guatemala. He was soundly defeated by the Pipil and also wounded in the process. A fresh attack was launched in 1525 and Alvarado subjugated the Pipil with abundant bloodshed. El Salvador thus became part of the Captaincy-General of Guatemala.

For more than two and a half centuries, El Salvador remained a quiet backwater because of an absence of any possibilites of exploitation that might bring quick riches. Meanwhile Spanish settlers arrived in the country and intermarried with Indians, creating a mixed race which forms the vast majority of the population today. The biggest export crop was indigo, used as a dye until the middle of the 19th century, when this was replaced by coffee.

■ Independence and Conflict: 1800-1930

Early in the 19th century, a wave of revolt spread across the Spanish colonies, and in 1811 José Matias Delgado, a Salvadoran priest, led an uprising, which was suppressed by loyalist troops. Independence from Spain finally came on September 15, 1821, the same date as in Guatemala, Honduras, Nicaragua and Costa Rica. For the next two years Central America was controlled by the Mexican emperor, Agustín de Iturbide. In 1822 a group of Salvadorans petitioned the United States for statehood, but the U.S. Congress declined to act on the request. In 1823 Mexican rule was repulsed and the United Provinces of Central America came into being, bringing together the five young republics. This federation met harsh opposition from powerful political, clerical and military factions, and it disintegrated gradually during the 1830s. It was to be a harbinger of failed efforts in later eras to build political or economic union in Central America.

Much of the 19th century was marked by political struggles between conservatives, who wished to retain the semi-feudal institutions bequeathed by the Spanish, and liberals, who favoured removal of feudal privileges enjoyed by big landowners and by portions of the clergy. Francisco Morazán, the Honduran who struggled to maintain Central American unity, was overthrown by the Guatemalan despot Rafael Carrera, who allied himself with conservative and clerical factions. After installing army commander Francisco Malespín as president of El Salvador in 1840, Carrera held indirect control over the country until his death in 1863. The latter half of the century was a period of extreme political instability, with countless military coups and revolutionary proclamations. At least two presidents met death by firing squad.

This period also marked the consolidation of the large family-owned agricultural estates, which were to plague Salvadoran society for many generations. Most of the communal and Indian lands, accounting for close to half the national territory, were converted to private property by force of arms during a four-decade period, and the power of the famed 14 families was born. These families came to own most of the country's wealth, and they held sway over the army and many of the politicians. Concentration of wealth was diluted gradually in the course of the 20th century as the number of wealthy families grew, but even in the 1980s it was possible to identify about 100 families whose holdings of land, industry and commerce dwarfed those of the rest of society and another 200 or so who controlled much of the rest.

■ Seeds of Revolt: 1930-1979

The heavy concentration of land ownership resulting from the confiscation of communal lands created a proletarian rural labour force, which came closer than in most other countries to exemplifying the Marxist notion of an army of job-seekers exploited by a powerful oligarchy. The onset of the Great Depression in 1929 caused a calamitous decline in world coffee prices, which in turn led to a sharp reduction in rural wages. This spawned a revolt in 1932 headed by the leader of the tiny Communist party, Agustín Farabundo Martí, the son of Indian peasants. His name would later be adopted by the rebel front which coalesced in the late 1970s.

Meanwhile, a presidential election in 1931 had produced inconclusive results, and political confusion ensued. Gen. Maximiliano Hernández Martínez seized power in 1932, moving brutally to end the rural revolt and slaughtering an estimated 30,000 people in what became known as *la matanza*, the slaughter. Indians were singled out for even harsher persecution and, as a matter of self-protection, had to abandon their traditional dress and the use of their language in public places, making their assimilation almost complete. Gen. Hernández was overthrown in 1944, but military rule was firmly entrenched and would continue for another generation in close alliance with the landowning oligarchy, who had been shaken by the 1932 revolt and supported tough military vigilance.

Because of overcrowding and the unavailability of suitable land, many Salvadoran peasants emigrated to neighbouring countries. By 1969 it was estimated that 300,000 Salvadorans were living illegally in Honduras, with its lower population density. They were resented as intruders by some Hondurans. Rioting erupted at an international soccer match, and Honduran mobs attacked Salvadoran immigrants. Tensions increased to the point that the two countries went briefly to war in what some journalists dubbed the Footbal War. A truce was signed two weeks later, but not before several thousand people had been killed, and even today there remain contested pockets of land in the mountain areas along the border.

Growing political unrest in El Salvador in the 1970s was greeted with renewed repression and blatant fraud in the 1972 and 1977 elections. Since 1961, the dominant political party had been the *Partido de Conciliación Nacional* (PCN), which acted as a front for a series of military dictators until the last of them, Gen. Carlos Humberto Romero, was overthrown in a 1979 coup. The coup leaders installed a civilian-military junta that began to undertake land reform and other measures aimed at drawing popular support away from the growing revolutionary movement. Distressed by the radicalism of some of the measures proposed by the new junta, more conservative elements in the army staged a counter-coup in 1980, repressing protests with great brutality and moving the country to full-scale civil war.

■ **Civil War: 1979-1992**

Left-wing guerrilla forces began small-scale military operations in the late 1970s and created joint political structures. The five guerrilla armies forming the *Frente Farabundo Martí de Liberación Nacional* (FMLN) each maintained a degree of autonomy, but they also undertook many joint actions, vastly increasing the scale of their anti-government campaign in 1980. In 1979, the smaller *Frente Sandinista de Liberación Nacional* in nearby Nicaragua had dislodged the half-century-old U.S.-backed Somoza family dictatorship, and there were fears in San Salvador and

Washington that this left-wing triumph could repeat itself elsewhere in Central America.

With guerrilla activity on the rise, the Salvadoran army became heavily dependent on military supplies and financial help from the United States, reluctantly turning the government over to civilian control under pressure from Washington. In January 1981, two pivotal events unfolded: the rebel forces of the FMLN staged what they prematurely called their final offensive, launching a coordinated series of attacks that actually fell far short of their objectives; and Ronald Reagan entered the White House in Washington, bringing with him a virulent anti-communism, an obsession with Central America, and the notion that rebel activity there was manipulated from Havana and ultimately from Moscow. The Reagan administration made clear its determination to prevent a rebel triumph in El Salvador, but it had to contend with a Democrat-controlled Congress which made military aid conditional on social progress and improvements in El Salvador's sordid human rights record. Notable among U.S. concerns were the notorious right-wing death squads, linked informally with the army, whose thousands of victims included Archbishop Oscar Romero of San Salvador, gunned down in 1980 while celebrating mass.

To obtain congressional support for its increasingly massive aid to the anti-communist government of El Salvador, the Reagan administration had to engineer modest political and economic reforms there, and its chosen tool was the centre-right Christian Democratic Party, led by José Napoleón Duarte, who won the 1984 presidential election with overt U.S. support. (Duarte had won the most votes in the 1972 presidential election but was cheated of victory through massive fraud. He was forced into exile in Venezuela, returning only after the 1979 coup.) His chief opponent in 1984 was Roberto D'Aubuisson, a cashiered army major closely linked with death squad activity and leader of the far-right *Alianza Republicana Nacional* (National Republican Alliance, known by its Spanish acronym ARENA). The political left boycotted the 1984 election for fear of repression.

Duarte was placed in an impossible position. His own instincts leaned toward pursuing the ambitious land reform program that existed on paper and bringing other changes to the structure of Salvadoran society, but he was thwarted in his aims by the government's financial weakness and by the Reagan administration's insistence on a military solution. He also faced fierce opposition from entrenched economic interests and the enormous power acquired by the military, partly as a result of heavy infusions of cash and weapons from the U.S. Nor was he able to pursue serious peace talks with the FMLN.

Meanwhile, the civil war ground on inconclusively, claiming thousands of victims each year, creating hundreds of thousands of internal refugees, and ravaging the economy. Neither side could gain the upper hand, however. The FMLN was not nearly powerful enough to seize control of the government, but it remained strong enough to prevent the army from establishing positions in rebel-held territory, and it launched random attacks in other areas, including a large-scale assault on San Salvador in 1989. The U.S. maintained a small contingent of military advisors to El Salvador throughout the 1980s and made modest strides in professionalizing the armed forces, but it achieved only limited success in purging the Salvadoran army of some of its more egregious human rights violators. Among the better documented army-linked atrocities were the murders of six Jesuit priests in 1989.

■ **Arrival of Peace: 1992-present**

In the 1989 election, voters showed their displeasure with the ineptitude and corruption that had marked Christian Democratic rule and chose the new ARENA leader, Alfredo Cristiani, as president. This apparent rightward shift brought little perceptible change in the day-to-day actions of the government.

During the long years of the Salvadoran dispute, leaders of various Latin American countries attempted on several occasions to mediate and to bring about peace talks. The rebels also had floated various peace proposals, but these failed in large part because of army insistence on full rebel disarmament and rebel insistence on the dismissal of key army commanders. In 1990 an agreement on human rights monitors was reached under United Nations auspices, and on January 16, 1992, the Salvadoran government and the FMLN finally signed a peace agreement and achieved a formal truce. Both sides, it seems, were simply tired of fighting.

The agreement included schedules for the demobilization of rebel forces, the dismantling of five army elite units, land allotments for ex-fighters, and the creation of a United Nations observer force. At several points each side accused the other of failing to respect the agreement, but the truce held. In March 1993 there appeared to be a serious violation of the spirit of the agreement when, just days after a UN commission released its report on human rights violations, the government issued a blanket amnesty for the guilty parties, including many high-ranking army officers.

In the 1994 elections, ARENA retained power, with Armando Calderón Sol as its presidential candidate, but for the first time the FMLN participated directly and obtained nearly one-third of the votes. It prepared to play the role of loyal opposition, and one of its first moves was to achieve the removal of a corrupt old guard from the top ranks of the judiciary and their replacement with better qualified jurists. El Salvador appeared headed toward a strengthening of political pluralism and judicial independence.

Politics

El Salvador has a long tradition of political intolerance, and opposition groups have been banned or physically suppressed at several points in history. In the 1970s, the political system again proved incapable of dealing with dissent by any means other than repression or electoral fraud. This led to the formation of the left-wing *Frente Farabundo Martí de Liberación Nacional* (FMLN), which took up armed struggle in 1979. For more than 12 years the country endured a devastating civil war until a United Nations-brokered peace agreement led to a formal and lasting truce early in 1992.

Naturally, political matters remain a very touchy subject in El Salvador, and many people have strong feelings. But there appears to be a growing respect for political pluralism, and people seem willing to discuss politics far more readily than they did during the more repressive wartime era. Still, visitors to El Salvador today should listen with respect when a conversation turns to politics and offer opinions only when asked.

The FMLN converted itself to a political party and presented candidates in the 1994 national elections. Although several of its candidates and organizers were killed, the campaign was far less violent than many people had feared, and the FMLN was able to hold public rallies and conduct other electoral activities far more openly than anyone could have imagined possible only a few years earlier. The *Convergencia Democrática*, a party loosely allied with the FMLN, had presented candidates in 1989 but was able to run only a very limited campaign.

The most powerful political party is ARENA, the acronym for *Alianza Republicana Nacional* (National Republican Alliance). This party was led at its founding by Roberto D'Aubuisson, a charismatic but troubled figure who was broadly suspected of involvement in death squad activities. ARENA was allied with wealthy business interests and favoured a very hard line against the FMLN, but after coming to power in the 1989 election, with coffee plantation owner Alfredo Cristiani as its presidential candidate, it mellowed and ended up signing a peace agreement. ARENA was returned to power in the 1994 election, led by Armando Calderón Sol, a former mayor of San Salvador.

The *Partido Democracia Cristiana* (Christian Democratic Party) was cheated of electoral victory by massive fraud in 1972 and again in 1977. Finally in 1984 the party was able to assume power after José Napoleón Duarte won the presidential election. Duarte's five years in power were a gloomy period, with the death and destruction wrought by war, constant interference from Washington, an army that seemed to pay little heed to the wishes of its civilian masters, and a series of corruption scandals. Duarte died of cancer shortly after leaving office. Since then the party has been riven by internal conflict.

The *Partido de Conciliación Nacional* acted as a political front for a series of military dictators who ruled between 1961 and 1979. Since then it has had only a minor presence.

The Salvadoran president is elected for a five-year term and is barred by the constitution from seeking re-election. If no presidential candidate wins more than half the votes cast, a run-off election is held between the two top contenders. El Salvador has an 84-seat legislative assembly which is elected by proportional representation. The country is divided for administrative purposes into 14 departments, and it has 262 municipalities, each with an elected mayor.

The first round of the 1994 presidential election was held on March 20. Armando Calderón Sol of ARENA won 49.3 % of the vote, Rubén Zamora of the FMLN 25.6%, and Christian Democrat Fidel Chávez Mena 16%, with other candidates splitting the remaining nine per cent. In the run-off, held on April 24, Calderón was elected with 68.2% while Zamora got 31.6%.

In the legislative assembly, ARENA won 39 seats, the FMLN 21, the Christian Democrats 18, the *Partido de Conciliación Nacional* four, *Convergencia Democrática* one, and one seat was undetermined. ARENA won 200 of the

262 mayoralties. Among the FMLN members of the assembly, some are former guerrilla fighters.

In the first round of voting, the FMLN complained that as many as 300,000 of the 2.4 million eligible voters were prevented from voting because of problems with voting lists or the loss of documents, but it agreed to accept the results after attempts were made to correct some of the problems before the second round.

Economy

For much of its modern history El Salvador has endured economic structures that have been more feudalist than capitalist. Concentrations of land ownership have created great extremes of wealth and poverty. A land reform program designed by American advisors during the administration of Jimmy Carter was initiated in 1980 and broke up the very largest estates, but the political will to press forward seemed to evaporate as the program moved into its second phase, which would have broken up some of the other big estates. Land was purchased by the government and distributed to newly formed peasant cooperatives, but later some of the cooperatives were encouraged to dissolve and divide the land into individual farms.

About 40 per cent of Salvadoran territory is suited to agriculture, and until 1980 most of this land was owned by just two per cent of the population even though farming absorbed nearly half the workforce. In conjunction with land reform, the government nationalized the banking industry and some export firms in an attempt to remove them from the control of the landowning oligarchy and thus to make farm credit more widely available.

Coffee is the most important export crop, and very high yields are obtained in El Salvador's rich volcanic soils. Coffee-growing takes patience and financial strength since the plants can take five years to mature. It grows best at middle altitudes, particularly in shaded areas. Cotton is cultivated in hot, damp areas along the coast and also in the low interior valleys, typically on large agricultural estates. Pesticides are used heavily, leaching into the sea in some places in high enough concentrations to affect catches of fish and shrimp. Sugarcane is grown on the plateaus and the inland valleys, while cattle and hogs are raised on poorer land. New export crops have been developed, including sesame, poppyseed, tropical flowers and certain fruits and vegetables. Shrimp farming has grown quickly in importance. The main subsistence crops are maize, beans and sorghum. Even today many peasants work tiny plots of land and have barely enough resources to survive until the next harvest.

With its very small land area and concentration of agricultural resources on more lucrative export crops, El Salvador has to import about one-quarter of its basic food supply. This heavy dependence on farm exports means the country is buffeted periodically by swings in world commodity prices, especially of coffee. Exporters have to be well capitalized. Some of El Salvador's great family fortunes were created by coffee in the latter half of the 19th century when the government banned the traditional Indian communal lands and offered land to coffee planters. Tough vagrancy laws prohibited idleness, and peasants were rounded up to work on the plantations, usually at derisory wages.

Salvadorans have a reputation for being hard workers, and the country has the highest concentration of manufacturing in Central America, consisting mostly of light industry such as the production of textiles, clothing, shoes, rubber goods, furniture, construction materials and basic implements. There is also some production of industrial chemicals, fertilizers and pharmaceuticals. Some of the industrial textiles are quite sophisticated. The country had also begun to develop an electronics assembly industry; this sector was stymied by the war but has started to grow again. Most of El Salvador's industrial exports go to other Central American countries. There is also a small mining industry. The tourism industry is in its infancy and does not yet play an important economic role.

Society and Culture

■ **Race, Income and Religion**

Accurate figures are hard to come by, but it is estimated that more than 90 per cent of El Salvador's nearly six million people are of mixed European and Amerindian race, known as *mestizos*. Of the remainder, most are people of pure (or almost pure) European descent or of pure (or almost pure) Amerindian descent. Although racial discrimination is no longer practised formally, people with paler skins often tend to be wealthier and better educated.

Salvadoran society is stratified less along racial lines than along income lines. The gap between wealthy and poor remains cavernous. A visitor who sees only the more prosperous neighbourhoods in San Salvador could come away with the impression that this is somehow an extension of California, although it is hard to miss some of the mud and cardboard huts on the outskirts of the city. Recent decades have seen the emergence of a stronger middle class, composed largely of professional and technical workers and small business owners. As this middle class grows, income distribution will no longer be quite as lopsided.

El Salvador does not have as clear a cultural identity as some other Latin American countries. This probably has much to do with the high degree of assimilation among the remaining Amerindian inhabitants. In neighbouring Guatemala, by way of contrast, the country's cultural identity is closely connected with its Amerindian majority, particularly in matters of music, dress, language and religious worship.

Spanish is the sole official language of El Salvador and is spoken everywhere. In a few villages and small towns, Nahua is also spoken by some Native people.

Roman Catholicism is the dominant religion. In recent years Protestant Evangelical and Baptist groups, many of them U.S.-based, have made substantial inroads. The Catholic church in El Salvador used to be very conservative, but this has changed in the last generation. Important elements in the church were influenced by liberation theology and chose to identify themselves with the poor. This alienated many of the church's wealthy patrons. Perhaps the most visible reminder of this is the harshly austere cathedral in San Salvador, left in an ugly, unfinished state as funds to complete the building work simply dried up. Archbishop Oscar Arnulfo Romero, assassinated in 1980, is revered as a martyr by most Salvadorans but reviled as a traitor by some people on the political right.

Arts and Leisure

Poetry is very popular in El Salvador, and Roque Dalton, who died as the result of a factional dispute among guerrillas, was one of the country's most renowned poets. Horacio Castellanos Moya is the most noted contemporary novelist. His novel *La Diáspora* has won several awards, and his work also includes books of short stories.

U.S. pop music and Latin musical forms such as salsa, merengue and Mexican *ranchero* songs dominate the radio airwaves and the handful of night clubs in operation. Before and especially during the war years Salvadorans developed a semi-underground tradition of *canción popular*, or folk songs, accompanied by guitar and often conveying political messages. The guitar is the most common musical instrument.

Many towns and villages celebrate festivals or saint's days with masked processions, exuberant costumes, and musical bands. There are also many processions during Holy Week, the period immediately preceeding Easter. The most noteworthy of these processions take place in the city of Sonsonate, in the southwest of El Salvador.

The town of La Palma in the north is the birthplace of an artistic tradition centred around simple, brightly coloured images of rural life. These images find their way onto painted wooden objects, jewellery boxes, ceramic items, and industrial textiles in the form of towels and bathrobes. Several other towns have become noted for their handicrafts, including Nahuizalco for basketware, Ilobasco for ceramics and Chalchuapa for masks. Many of these objects can be purchased in San Salvador.

No survey of Salvadoran culture is complete without mention of *el fútbol* (soccer), by far the most popular sport but, more than that, an obsession. It accounts for much of the leisure time of young men who play the game and older men who listen to broadcasts of professional matches. Many women also get lured into following the game.

El Salvador in Statistics

Most figures here are drawn from the *Human Development Report 1994* compiled by the United Nations Development Programme.

Land area: 21,041 km² (8,115 mi²)
Population (1994 estimate): 5.8 million
Average population density per km² (1994): 276
Urban residents as proportion of total (1992): 45%
Average annual population growth rate (1960-92): 2.4%
Average annual population growth rate (1992-2000, estimate): 2.2%
Gross domestic product (1991): US$5.9 billion
Average annual growth in GDP per capita (1980-91): -0.3%
Average annual growth in GDP per capita (1965-80): +1.5%
Annual inflation (1992): 10%
Average annual inflation (1980-91): 17.4%
Proportion of urban people living in absolute poverty (1980-90): 20%
Proportion of rural people living in absolute poverty (1980-90): 75%
Proportion of labour force in agriculture (1990-92): 11%
Proportion of labour force in industry (1990-92): 23%
Proportion of labour force in services (1990-92): 66%
Proportion of labour force composed of women (1990-92): 45%
Life expectancy at birth (1992): 65.2 years
Life expectancy at birth (1960): 50.5 years
Life expectancy at birth among females (1992): 68.2
Proportion of population with access to health services (1992): 60%
Proportion of total population with access to safe water (1992): 47%
Proportion of rural population with access to safe water (1992): 19%
People without access to health services (1992): 2.2 million
People without access to safe water (1992): 2.8 million
Infant mortality rate per 1,000 births (1992): 46
Infant mortality rate per 1,000 births (1960): 130
Adult literacy rate (1992): 74.6%
Adult literacy rate (1970): 57.0%
Average years of schooling (1992): 4.2
Illiterate male adults (1992): 0.2 million
Illiterate female adults (1992): 0.5 million
School-age children not attending school (1992): 379,000
Fertility rate (1992): 4.2 children per woman
Fertility rate (1960): 6.9 children per woman
Average age of women at first marriage (1980-90): 19.4 years
Proportion of couples using contraceptives (1985-92): 47%
Average caloric intake (1991): 102% of daily requirements
Malnourished children under five (1992): 153,000
Motor vehicles per 100 people (1989-90): 2.2
Rank of El Salvador in the UN human development index: 112th of 173 countries

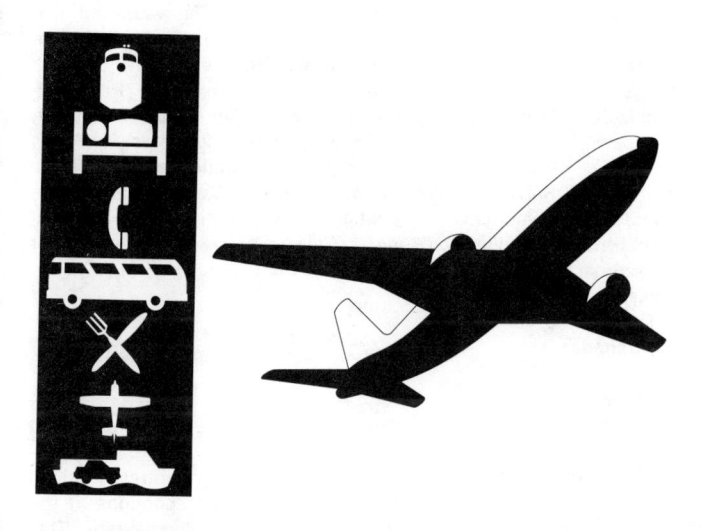

PRACTICAL INFORMATION

Visitors can travel freely throughout El Salvador, but planning is a good idea. This section is intended to help you organize your visit to El Salvador by providing general information and practical advice.

Entrance Formalities

■ **Passports and Visas**

All visitors to El Salvador must hold valid passports (except citizens of Guatemala, Honduras, Nicaragua or Costa Rica, who can show national identity cards instead; the same applies to Salvadorans living abroad).

Citizens of many countries also require visas or tourist cards to enter El Salvador. Regulations can change without notice, and it is wise to check ahead with a Salvadoran embassy or consulate. A list appears below. If you are going on a package tour, the tour operator should be able to provide information on entry requirements.

Normally, no photos are required to obtain visas or tourist cards, and the procedure should not take more than a few minutes, although this can vary from one embassy (or consulate) to the next. Most provide visas and other consular services only in the morning and early afternoon. It is best to phone ahead.

Entry documents normally are valid for stays of up to 90 days. Extensions for up to 90 days more can be obtained at the *Dirección General de Migración* (General Directorate of Immigration) in the *Centro de Gobierno* (Government Centre) on Avenida Juan Pablo II in San Salvador.

The Government of El Salvador has long-standing bilateral agreements with a number of countries, including the United States and most western European countries, easing or eliminating visa requirements. There is no comparable agreement with Canada.

Citizens of the **United States** can obtain visas free of charge, valid for multiple entries for ten years from the date of issue, from any Salvadoran embassy or consulate. Alternately, they can obtain a tourist card for $10, valid for a single entry, upon arrival in El Salvador, whether by air, land or sea.

Citizens of **Canada** or **Mexico** can obtain a tourist card for $10 (U.S. currency), valid for a single entry, upon arrival in El Salvador, whether by air, land or sea. Alternately, they can obtain single-entry visas for $30 (U.S. currency) from Salvadoran embassies or consulates. This latter alternative offers no perceptible advantage.

Citizens of most countries in **Western Europe** other than France can enter El Salvador without a visa or tourist card. Only a valid passport is required. This includes citizens of Britain, Germany, Holland, Belgium, Switzerland, Austria, Italy, Spain, Sweden and Denmark. Citizens of **France** require consular visas. Single-entry visas cost $30 and may be obtained from any Salvadoran embassy or consulate. (France ended the reciprocal agreement on visa-free entry it used to have with El Salvador.)

Citizens of **Australia, New Zealand,** and virtually all countries in **Asia, Africa,** and **Eastern Europe** require consular visas, obtainable for $30 from Salvadoran embassies and consulates. Citizens of most countries in **South America** and the **Caribbean** also require visas. Citizens of **Colombia** are an exception: they require only valid passports. Citizens of **Israel** require consular visas, but there is no fee.

Customs

Border formalities are much faster than they used to be. With improving economic relations among Central American countries, customs inspections at the land borders have become rare. This does not necessarily make things easier for smugglers, because the neighbouring countries also have fairly rigid regulations. Visitors to El Salvador may bring a reasonable of quantity of clothing and items such as photographic or electronic equipment for personal use.

■ Alcohol and Tobacco

Visitors 18 years or older may bring up to 1.5 litres (50 ounces) of liquor plus 1.5 litres (50 ounces) of wine, and either three cartons of cigarettes or one kilogram (2.2 pounds) of tobacco. Gifts totalling not more than $100 in value may enter duty-free.

■ Fruits, Vegetables, Plants and Leather

Severe restrictions apply to food items. With very few exceptions, meat or dairy products are subject to immediate seizure. Tinned meats from the U.S., Australia, New Zealand and a handful of other countries are exempt provided they have been heat-sterilized and de-boned. Fruits are subject to examination by sanitary inspectors and may be seized if they do not pass muster. Plants and flowers must be free of earth and will be examined and treated at a quarantine station. Leather goods and animal skins from tropical countries where certain livestock diseases are endemic are prohibited.

■ **Pets**

Conditions for the entry of dogs, cats and other domestic animals are so rigid that only the most determined of pet-owners will bother. Before entering, pets must be vaccinated against a long list of diseases and hold a certificate issued by a veterinarian. That's not all. A permit is required from the *Ministerio de Agricultura y Ganadería* (Ministry of Agriculture and Livestock) in San Salvador, and this can take a long time to obtain. Further information is available from Salvadoran embassies and consulates.

■ **Firearms**

Firearms and ammunition cannot be brought in except with a special permit from the *Ministerio de Defensa y Seguridad Pública* (Ministry of Defence and Public Security) in San Salvador. Narcotics are prohibited at all times. Visitors carrying a large quantity of pharmaceutical products should make sure they have prescription labels or some other way of indicating that they are strictly for personal medical use.

■ **Cars**

Motorists must have proof of ownership of the vehicle they are driving and a valid driver's licence issued in their country of residence. Insurance is not required. Foreign-registered vehicles may not remain in the country more than 30 days unless authorization is obtained from customs authorities.

■ **Exports**

Anything may be exported from El Salvador with the exception of archeological pieces, antiques, and gold or silver bullion.

Embassies and Consulates

■ **Foreign Embassies and Consulates in San Salvador**

Please note that honorary consulates, for instance in the case of Canada, can provide only limited services.

Belgium
Final 65ª Avenida Sur 3415-A
☎ 224-5382, 223-7343

Belize
Condominio Médico B, local 5,2º piso
Boulevard Tutunichapa,
Urbanización La Esperanza
☎ 226-3588

Canada
Avenida Las Palmas 111,
Colonia San Benito
☎ 279-3290

Costa Rica
Alameda Roosevelt 3107,
Edificio La Centroamericana
☎ 223-0273

France
1ª Calle Poniente 3718,
Colonia Escalón
☎ 279-4014

Germany
Avenida República Federal de Alemania
163, Colonia Escalón
☎ 298-3439

Great Britain
Paseo Escalón 4828
☎ 298-1763, 298-1769, 298-1455

Guatemala
15ª Avenida Norte 135
☎ 222-2903

Honduras
1ª Calle Poniente 4326,
Colonia Escalón
☎ 223-3856

Mexico
Calle Circunvalación y Pasaje #12,
Colonia San Benito
☎ 298-1176, 298-1034, 298-1079

Nicaragua
71ª Avenida Norte y 1ª Calle Poniente,
Colonia Escalón
☎ 224-1223, 224-0979, 223-7729
223-9860

Netherlands
Final Calle La Mascota,
Urbanización Maquilishut,
Edificio Lotisa
☎ 223-4000

Panama
Alameda Roosevelt y 55ª Avenida Norte,
Edificio Copa
☎ 271-0162

Spain
Calle La Reforma 164,
Colonia San Benito
☎ 298-1188

Switzerland
Paseo Escalón 4363
☎ 223-1645

United States
Boulevard Santa Elena,
Antiguo Cuscatlán
☎ 278-4444

■ Embassies and Consulates of El Salvador Abroad

Belgium
Avenue de Tervuren 171, 7e étage
Bruxelles
☎ (2) 733-0485

Belize
11 Handyside St.
Belize City
☎ (2) 78158

Canada
4330 - rue Sherbrooke O.
Montréal, QC
☎ (514) 934-3678

209 - Kent St.
Ottawa, ON
☎ (613) 238-2939

292 Sheppard Ave. W. #200
Toronto, ON
☎ (416) 512-8195, 512-8140

Costa Rica
Final Avenida 10 #3370, entre 33ª y 35ª Calles,
Barrio Los Yoses
San José
☎ 253861, 249034

Embassies and Consulates

France
12, rue Galilée
Paris
☎ (1) 47.23.98.23, 47.20.42.02

Germany
Adenauralee 238
Bonn
☎ (228) 549913, 549914

Great Britain
5, Great James Street
London
☎ (71) 430-2141

Guatemala

18ª Calle 14-30, Zona 13
Guatemala City
☎ (2) 326421, 325421, 322449

16ª Calle 3-20, Zona 3
Escuinta

Honduras

Calzada República del Uruguay,
Casa 19, Colonia San Carlos
Tegucigalpa
☎ 367344, 368045

Edificio Rivera y Compañía, 5° piso,
Local 218
San Pedro Sula

2ª Avenida Sureste,
esquina con 5ª Calle Sureste,
Barrio San Andrés
Nuevo Ocotepeque

Calle Colón, Casa 117,
Barrio El Centro
Choluteca
☎ 820744, 822871

Mexico

Paseo de Las Palmas 1003,
Lomas de Chapultepec
Mexico City, D.F.
☎ (5) 596-7493, 596-7366

Prologación Avenida de Las Palmas,
Manzana 35, Casa No. L 8-C,
Fraccionamiento Los Laureles
Tapachula
☎ (962) 64822

Netherlands
Catsheuvel 117,
Ka's Gravenhage
The Hague
☎ (70) 352-0712

Nicaragua
Km 9½, Carretera a Masaya,
Residencial Las Colinas,
Pasaje Los Cerros 142
Managua
☎ 760712

Panamá
Edificio Citibank #408,
Villa España
Panamá City
☎ 233020

Switzerland
65, rue de Lausanne
Geneva
☎ (22) 732-7036

United States

46 Park Ave., 2nd floor
New York, NY
☎ (212) 889-3608, 889-3609

2308 California St. N.W.
Washington, D.C.
☎ (202) 265-7671

104 S. Michigan Ave. #423
Chicago, IL
☎ (312) 332-1393, 332-1394

300 Biscayne Blvd. Way #1020
Miami, FLA
☎ (305) 371-8850

1136 World Trade Center
New Orleans, LA
☎ (504) 522-4266

6420 Hillcroft #100
Houston, TX
☎ (713) 270-6239, 270-0015

2412 W. 7th St., 2nd floor
Los Angeles, CA
☎ (213) 383-6134

870 Market St. #508
San Francisco, CA
☎ (415) 781-7924, 781-7925

Elsewhere

El Salvador has embassies in Kingston (Jamaica), Santo Domingo, Caracas, Bogotá, Quito, Lima, Santiago de Chile, Buenos Aires, Montevideo, Brasilia and Asunción, as well as in Milan, Rome, Madrid, Tokyo, Seoul, Taipei and Jerusalem. It also has a consulate near San Juan (Puerto Rico) and honorary consulates in Stockholm, Auckland, Hong Kong and Calcutta.

❓ Tourist Information

Salvadoran embassies and consulates abroad are able to provide only very limited tourism information.

The *Instituto Salvadoreño de Turismo*, a government body, is responsible for tourism promotion. Its main office is in the centre of San Salvador *(Mon to Fri 8 a.m. to 4 p.m., Calle Rubén Darío 619 between 9ª and 11ª Avenidas Sur, phone 222-8000 or 222-0960)*. Staff can provide material in Spanish and English on tourist attractions as well as practical information on matters such as buses. They also provide crude mimeographed maps of the city and country. Some staff members seem better informed than others.

The *Instituto* has a branch office at the international airport *(open every day 8 a.m. to 5 p.m.)*. There are no tourism offices elsewhere in the country. The staff at some hotels are helpful, and outside San Salvador they may sometimes be indispensable as a source of information.

It is difficult to find good maps. Some hotels offer better maps than the tourism office. The best maps of El Salvador and of the capital are wall maps produced and sold by the *Instituto Geográfico Nacional*, located at Avenida Juan Vertiz 79 in the Ciudad Delgado district of San Salvador. Its procedures are very bureaucratic.

■ Turicentros

Because the war kept most foreign tourists away for many years, the *Instituto Salvadoreño de Turismo* has concentrated most of its efforts on internal tourism. Besides providing information to tourists, the *Instituto* operates a series of parks around the country with wooded grounds, swimming pools, eating places and other facilities. Called *turicentros*, these parks charge modest admission fees and enable Salvadorans to enjoy the outdoors. Foreigners are always welcome.

■ Organized Tours

The *Instituto* also offers numerous one-day and two-day weekend bus tours from San Salvador to various rivers, beaches, mountains, *turicentros* and points of cultural interest. Fares are very cheap, typically about $2 for a one-day excursion. Tickets should be purchased in advance. Full information is available from the *Instituto*'s main office. The programs change each week.

Several privately-run tour companies in San Salvador offer tours to various parts of the country with comfortable vehicles and more lavish attention. These companies include **Pullmantur**, Condominio Balam Quitze, Paseo Escalón y 89ª Avenida, local 4-B, ☎ 279-4166, and **Nanch Tours**, which has offices in the Camino Real, Presidente and El Salvador hotels. Prices depend on the number of participants.

Some air-and-hotel packages offer participants optional tours which can be purchased after arrival in El Salvador. Some also include visits to Guatemala or Honduras.

Entering the Country

■ By Air

The *Aeropuerto Internacional de El Salvador* (El Salvador International Airport) is located near the small town of Comalapa about 40 km (25 mi) south of San Salvador. There is a good four-lane highway to the capital but no regular bus service. Taxis charge about $15, and rental cars are available. Avis, Budget and Hertz are all represented.

The airport is located conveniently for those who are headed to resorts on the Costa del Sol. Flight information is available from the individual airlines.

Privately owned **TACA** (*Transportes Aéreos Centro Américanos*) is the Salvadoran national airline and the most powerful force in Central American commercial aviation. It has daily flights from each of the other Central American countries and from New York, Washington, Miami, New Orleans, Houston, Los Angeles, San Francisco and Mexico City.

Other airlines serving El Salvador include **United Airlines** from Miami, Los Angeles and Mexico City, **American Airlines** and **Iberia** from Miami, and **Continental Airlines** from Houston. All provide connections to and from Europe, and all except Iberia offer connections throughout the United States. There are no direct flights from Europe.

Aviateca flies to El Salvador from Los Angeles, Chicago, New Orleans, Guatemala City, Managua, San José and Panama City, **LACSA** from San José, Mexico City and Los Angeles, and **COPA** from Panama City, San José, Managua and Guatemala City. Aviateca provides connections from Cancún and Flores (near Tikal), while both LACSA and COPA offer connections to and from South America and the Caribbean.

There is no direct scheduled air service between El Salvador and Canada, but **Royal Aviation** provides weekly charter flights from Montréal most of the year. Tickets on charter flights can be purchased only through travel agents.

Though charter companies such as Royal can provide lower rates, air fares to and from El Salvador tend to be fairly high. In a few instances there may be a significant saving in flying to Guatemala City and doing the last hop by road. A good travel agent can advise you.

An airport tax of $17 or its equivalent in colones applies to all departing passengers. This must be paid at check-in and can be a useful way of getting rid of unspent colones

■ By Car

El Salvador has good highway connections with both Guatemala and Honduras. It can also be reached in a few hours from Nicaragua or from the Mexican state of Chiapas. There are four important border crossings from Guatemala and two from Honduras. Traffic throughout Central America moves on the right.

From Guatemala City the shortest route leads to the Salvadoran border at Las Chinamas, and a secondary route goes via San Cristóbal. Travellers coming along the Pacific coastal plain of Guatemala or by the direct route from Tapachula will enter El Salvador at La Hachadura. Those arriving from Chiquimula or Esquipulas will enter at Anguiatú, in the northwestern corner of El Salvador.

From Tegucigalpa or Managua, the normal entry point is El Amatillo, while most travellers arriving from San Pedro Sula or Copán will enter at El Poy, just north of the enchanting town of La Palma, noted for its abundant production of quality handicrafts.

Travellers heading for El Salvador should plan their journeys so that they arrive at the border well before dusk. Because of security concerns, nighttime travel is not advised on Salvadoran highways.

■ By Bus

More than 20 buses a day travel in each direction between Guatemala City and San Salvador, many of them stopping also at Santa Ana, in western El Salvador. Most of these services are provided with superannuated Greyhound buses (minus the air conditioning and toilets) now embarked on a second career in Central America, but there are a few modern vehicles as well. All are far more comfortable than the very cramped buses used on routes within El Salvador. The one-way fare is about $5, and travel time is five to six hours, including border formalities. Passengers must disembark and proceed through immigration on both sides of the border. Several companies, among them **Galgos**, **Melva**, **Pezzarossi** and **Mermex**, provide a coordinated service with departures at least once hourly up to late afternoon. It is possible to travel the same day to San Salvador from Tapachula, in southern Mexico, with a connection in Guatemala City.

Luxury service is provided several times a day between Guatemala City and San Salvador by a company called **King Quality**. This company uses modern, air conditioned, toilet-equipped buses, and it serves light meals on board that are included in the one-way fare of $22 (or $40 round trip). An attendant handles all paperwork at the border, allowing passengers to remain on board. Travel time is four hours.

King Quality provides a similar luxury service between Tegucigalpa and San Salvador once daily at a one-way fare of $36 (or $60 round trip). Travel time is about seven hours. Its main competitor on this route is **Cruceros del**

Golfo, which provides ordinary service twice daily for about $15 each way, with longer delays at the border.

Tica-Bus is a Costa Rican company that covers the Central American isthmus from Panama City to Guatemala City. It provides same-day, same-bus service to San Salvador from Managua and two-day service from San José, with an overnight stop in Managua. It also operates to San Salvador from Guatemala City directly and from Tegucigalpa with a connection. Comfort is midway between King Quality and the other companies.

Travellers also have the option of using ordinary local buses to the border, crossing by foot, and catching another local bus on the other side. This is more economical, but it is also slow, tedious and uncomfortable.

For information on buses within the country, see page 37.

■ By Rail or Sea

No international passenger services are provided. It is possible — and expensive — to hire a small boat between the Nicaraguan port of Potosí and the Salvadoran port of La Unión across the Gulf of Fonseca. There are immigration offices in both places.

Insurance

No insurance is required to enter El Salvador, not even for motorists. Nonetheless, before leaving home, it may be a good idea to consider purchasing trip cancellation insurance, supplementary health insurance and theft insurance. Often all three are sold together as a package at moderate cost. These policies can be purchased through insurance brokers or travel agencies. Motorists may also breathe a little more easily if their vehicles are properly insured.

Trip cancellation insurance comes in handy if a traveller has to call off a trip for valid medical reasons or because of a death in the family. It covers any non-refundable payments to travel suppliers such as airlines and must be purchased at the same time as initial payment is made for air tickets or tour packages.

Supplementary health insurance will cover medical expenses that go beyond what travellers can claim from their regular government or private insurer. Many policies also provide for emergency evacuation or repatriation, including the cost of an air ambulance. Although hospital costs are low in El Salvador compared to those in many other countries, the bills can still pile up quickly.

Health

■ Vaccinations

No vaccinations are required to enter El Salvador except for people who have travelled recently in a country where yellow fever is endemic. There is minimal risk of malaria, and very few cases of cholera. Anyone who has special concerns about tropical disease should consult a vaccination clinic before leaving home.

Bacterial Disorders

Sanitary conditions in El Salvador are poorer than in more northerly climes, and tap water is not safe to drink because of high bacterial levels. Ice cubes made with unpurified water, or raw fruit or vegetables rinsed in unpurified water, will carry the same bacteria. Water that has been boiled or filtered is safer, and bottled water is sold in many food shops and pharmacies. Make sure the seal is not broken.

The most common symptom of bacterial disorder is a mild case of diarrhea. This usually is not serious, but it is always annoying. Those who are afflicted should drink plenty of liquids to avoid dehydration and avoid most solid foods, especially dairy products. Pepto-Bismol is a simple and often effective remedy. Pharmacists can suggest other remedies as well. One litre of bottled water mixed with one teaspoon of sugar and three teaspoons of salt will help rehydrate those who have severe cases.

If a case of diarrhea lasts more than a few days, consider seeking medical help. Visitors who come down with something more serious should ask their hotel or a foreign embassy to recommend a doctor.

Different people have different levels of resistance to bacteria. Those whose tolerance is weak should err on the side of caution. At the better hotels and restaurants, purified drinking water will be readily available, ice cubes and salads will be prepared hygienically, and visitors will generally be kept out of harm's way (though there are never any airtight guarantees).

But not everyone does all their eating and drinking at fancy hotels. At more humble spots, things to avoid include drinks that do not come bottled, drinks with ice cubes, raw seafood (cooked seafood is usually safe), salads, and fruit that may have been rinsed. As for street stalls, some items may be stored without refrigeration or kept warm at unsafe temperatures. Those who have lived or travelled extensively in tropical places can probably let their guard down a bit. Even so, it never hurts to be aware of the potential hazards.

Water and Alcohol

In warm climates the risk of dehydration is greater and it is therefore is a good idea to drink plenty of water. Bottled water is easy to find, and many hotels provide purified water in the rooms. Heavy alcohol consumption also causes dehydration. When very thirsty, try drinking a glass or two of water before hitting the beer. Those who plan to do any serious drinking should take some water both before and after. Among other things this can lessen the discomfort from a hangover.

The Sun

One hazard faced by many vacationers is sunburn, which is caused by ultraviolet rays. Many doctors warn that heavy exposure to these harmful rays also increases the risk of skin cancer later in life. To lessen both these risks, anyone headed for the beach should wear a hat and use sunscreen. Apply sunscreen 20 minutes before exposure and often during exposure. Do most of your sunning in the early morning or late afternoon, avoiding the stronger mid-day rays, especially the first couple of days when the skin is most sensitive. Even shaded spots may be bombarded by reflected rays from the sand or water,

Pharmacies and Clinics

Most pharmacies in El Salvador carry a broad range of medicines, and some drugs that are sold only by prescription in western countries, including basic antibiotics, are available over the counter. It is easy to find a pharmacy (*farmacia* in Spanish) in any of the larger towns. Prescription drug users should bring a good supply with them and carry it in their hand baggage on the airplane. A small first-aid kit can also be useful.

Medical clinics are scattered about the country but, except in the larger cities, facilities tend to be rudimentary. On the other hand, the cost of treatment is very low. Medical attention is more sophisticated (and more expensive) at private clinics and hospitals in San Salvador. Members of the wealthy elite sometimes travel to Houston for medical care.

Climate

El Salvador has a tropical climate with warm temperatures year-round. There are two seasons, a dry season running from November to April and a rainy season (often called *invierno*, meaning winter) from May to October, with a transitional period of several weeks at each end. Even during the rainy season there are many dry days, and it is often sunny in the morning. The rains are frequently concentrated between the mid-afternoon and early evening hours, often taking the form of brief but intense showers.

Temperatures vary according to altitude, with cooler, more pleasant weather in the mountain areas. In coastal areas temperatures are often moderated by sea breezes. In San Salvador, which lies inland at an altitude of 700 m (2200 ft.) above sea level, average daytime highs range between 29°C and 32°C (84°F to 90°F) while average minimum temperatures range between 16°C and 19°C (61°F to 66°F). April, May and June are the warmest months. Sunlight is intense everywhere in the country.

Packing

A basic rule of thumb for travel almost anywhere in the world is to take half the clothing and twice the money you expect to need. Those who plan to stay put during most of their visit can go ahead and pack that extra outfit or those heavy books. But anyone who expects to be moving around a lot may find the extra weight rather burdensome.

Travellers should think carefully about how much they really need to take with them. The availability of fast and inexpensive laundry service in most towns makes it unnecessary to pack vast amounts of clothing. El Salvador's tropical climate eliminates the need for heavy clothing, and even in high altitudes at night a light sweater is sufficient. It is better to avoid lugging around a winter overcoat and boots. Try to leave those at home if you can get to your flight without them.

When planning your travel wardrobe, try to strike a balance between the formal and the outrageously informal. Formal clothing is rarely necessary except for business travellers, while clothing that reveals more than the usual amount of flesh is fine for the beach but less acceptable elsewhere. Aim for something in the middle. T-shirts and shorts are not especially welcome at the better restaurants in San Salvador.

Other things to pack include a toiletries kit (again, eliminate unnecessary items — the weight can add up), a small first-aid kit, any prescription drugs you normally use (do not put these in checked baggage), a sunhat and sunscreen, a camera and film, a small alarm clock, a reasonable quantity of reading material and, for news buffs, a small short-wave radio.

Two small bags can often be easier to handle than a single big one. Try to leave a little extra space for any items purchased during the trip.

Safety and Security

Some people shy away from travel to El Salvador because they have the impression it is still a country at war. A 1992 peace agreement ended the fighting between government and rebel forces, and years later the agreement continues to hold. It is safe now to travel in areas which only a few years ago were the scenes of heavy fighting, particularly in eastern and northern parts of the country. Army roadblocks disappeared long ago.

On the other hand, some former soldiers and police officers, plus a few former guerrilla fighters, have not found civilian jobs but do have access to weapons and know how to use them. This has contributed to a crime wave which has many Salvadorans worried. Serious statistics are lacking, but 1993 and 1994 saw greater than usual numbers of armed assaults and other serious crimes, with money rather than politics the motive.

Few foreign visitors have fallen victim, and it is possible to help keep it that way with a few sensible precautions.

First, visitors may notice that few Salvadorans venture onto the highways late at night. Perhaps this is because of exaggerated fears, but visitors would be wise to follow suit and restrict out-of-town motoring to the daytime and early evening hours unless they are accompanied by people who know their way around.

Second, the larger cities and even a few smaller towns have areas that are dangerous at night, including the old central district of San Salvador. Anyone planning to go out at night to unfamiliar areas or along unfamiliar streets should consider taking taxis. Hotel staff normally can advise which areas are safe and which are not.

Third and most important, visitors should use basic common sense. This means not wearing expensive jewellery on the street. It also means not taking large amounts of money or other items of value to the beach and not leaving them in hotel rooms. Some hotels offer individual safety deposit boxes. Others can store valuables in the hotel safe. When on the move, travellers should keep valuables in a spot where they cannot easily be snatched. That means no exterior waistband pouches, which are gone with a snip of the scissors. Pouches worn under the clothing can be awkward but are more secure. It is best to avoid wandering into crowds: this can be an invitation to pickpockets or bag-snatchers. Also, cars should be parked in busy areas and the glove compartment left open to show that there is nothing inside worth stealing.

Most Salvadorans are honest and hospitable, and travellers who observe basic precautions are unlikely to encounter serious security problems. The newly formed *Policía Nacional Civil* (National Civilian Police) is professionally trained and better respected than the army-controlled police forces it replaces. Visitors who do run into problems should not hesitate to contact a police officer.

■ At the Beach

There are no lifeguards at Salvadoran beaches, and many beaches have strong undertows, which greatly increase the risk of drowning. Bathers should be very cautious about going into deep water.

Also, although the temptation may often be strong to wander great distances along deserted stretches of beach, visitors should be reminded that there is safety in numbers, and solitary beaches may not always be immune from acts of banditry.

■ Women Travellers

Women travelling alone should bear in mind that modern feminism has made only limited progress in El Salvador. They may encounter attitudes of *machismo* that would be seen as anachronistic in North America or Western Europe. Upon occasion women may encounter unwanted masculine attention. A firm but polite attitude is the best way to indicate that this interest is not shared. On the other hand, women will find many Salvadorans, both male and female, to be genuinely protective and concerned for their well-being. The usual warnings about avoiding dark streets, rough bars and immodest clothing all apply.

Transportation

■ By Car

A driver's licence issued in the visitor's country of origin is accepted in El Salvador. An international driver's licence is not required. Nor is insurance required, although it would probably be a good idea to check on coverage before leaving home. Note that the damage waiver for rental cars covered by some gold credit cards may not be valid in El Salvador.

Car Rentals

Car rentals are available only in San Salvador and at the international airport. See page 59 for a list of car rental agencies. When inquiring about rates, it is important to learn if taxes, insurance and free kilometres are included. Several type of vehicle are available, including four-wheel-drive vehicles. Note that the damage waiver for rental cars covered by some gold credit cards may not be valid in El Salvador. This should be verified before leaving home.

Highways

El Salvador has the densest and most comprehensive network of paved highways in Central America. The most important road is the **Carretera Panamericana** (Pan-American Highway), which crosses the country from east to west and also connects the three biggest cities. The eastern and western parts of the country are also linked by

> ### Addresses
>
> In Spanish, as in many other languages, addresses are shown with the street name first followed by the number. Thus, for example, a street address expressed as 36 Magnolia Street in English would, in Spanish, become Calle Magnolia 36. In a few cases, addresses are given as the distance along a highway. An address shown as km 4, Carretera a Santa Tecla, lies four kilometres along the highway to Santa Tecla.
>
> Some street addresses are followed by the name of the district. The abbreviation "Col." appears quite often. This does not stand for colonel, but rather for colonia, which means district or neighbourhood. In suburban areas the terms urbanización or fraccionamiento are often used.
>
> In some small towns, street names are not used much. Instead, directions are often given in reference to local landmarks.

the **Carretera del Litoral** (the so-called Coastal Highway) which runs parallel to the Pacific coast although it is some distance inland most of the way. The principal highways have route numbers, but these are rarely used and appear on very few signposts.

Most highways have just two lanes. The Carretera Panamericana has four lanes between San Salvador and Santa Ana, as well as along a couple of short stretches between San Salvador and San Miguel. The highway between San Salvador and the international airport also has four lanes.

Road conditions vary. In general, highways seem to be better maintained in the western part of the country. In the east there are more potholes, and this can result in slower speeds. Certain small towns and villages can be reached only by dirt roads. Some of these roads are suitable only for trucks or four-wheel drive vehicles, especially after heavy rains.

Few highways have posted speed limits, but rough or crowded road conditions often serve as effective deterrents to speeding. On broader stretches of some busy highways, three vehicles can pass on what are really two-lane roads, and it can be unnerving to see drivers overtaking others in the face of oncoming traffic.

Another hazard, particularly on more lightly travelled highways, is the casual attitude taken by livestock — and their owners. Cattle will not deviate from their path, and honking is useless. The only thing to do is to stop and wait until they have passed or, if they are walking straight along the highway in the same direction you are, to move slowly between them and try to form an opening. Hogs and chickens, on the other hand, will usually try to get out of the way.

Most highways are all but abandoned after dark because of fears of attack by bandits. Anyone travelling at night should inquire first about the safety of the planned route.

Distance chart

km/mi	La Union	La Libertad	San Miguel	San Salvador	Santa Ana	Sonsonate
La Libertad	190/119		159/99	31/19	80/50	76/47.5
La Union		190/119	47/29	183/114	246/154	244/153
San Miguel	47/29	159/99		136/85	199/124	197/123
San Salvador	183/114	31/19	136/85		63/39	61/38
Santa Ana	246/154	80/50	199/124	63/39		40/25
Sonsonate	244/153	76/47.5	197/123	61/38	40/25	

Taxis

Taxis are a very good way of getting around urban areas. Rates are generally moderate. Most trips within San Salvador, for example, cost $2 to $3. Taxis are not metered; they have fixed rates according to distance. Passengers may wish to ask the driver how much he charges before embarking. To avoid any uncertainty, decide upon a fare before embarking.

Taxis may seem at first glance to be an expensive and extravagant means of transport for out-of-town excursions, but for half-day trips they are often cheaper than renting cars, and the driver will know his way around better than most visitors would. Even for full-day trips, the fare may not be that much higher than the cost of a car rental, and think of the stress you avoid. When negotiating a fare, it is essential for the driver to understand clearly where you plan to go and how long you plan to stay.

Buses

Figures published by the United Nations indicate that the rate of vehicle ownership in El Salvador is only 2.2 per hundred people. Consequently, the vast majority of the population travels by bus as their primary means of transport.

Buses go almost everywhere, often with very frequent service and always at astoundingly low fares. But comfort and speed are not their key virtues.

Many buses resemble old U.S. school buses, which a few of them are. Seating is very cramped, with five passengers abreast — two on one side of the aisle and three on the other. Seat rows are squeezed so tightly together that anyone taller than the average 10-year-old may have trouble with their knees! The seated passengers, of course, are the lucky ones. Often, though by no means always, the aisles are jammed almost beyond belief with standing passengers. It used to be common, although it is rare now, to see large numbers of passengers riding on the roof as well. Large pieces of baggage are stowed either behind the last row of seats or, in some cases, on the roof.

Fares are paid on board the bus to conductors who come up and down the aisle. Fares are so low that small change is often sufficient, and even on longer trips fares rarely exceed a couple of U.S. dollars, working out to well under two U.S. cents per kilometre. **Payment is accepted only in colones**, the national currency. ehicles used in international service are sometimes rather ancient, but they tend to be far more comfortable than buses operating within El Salvador. Tickets to other countries must be purchased before boarding the bus. On some lightly travelled rural routes, service is provided not by buses but by pickup trucks, with passengers standing on the rear platform. This does not score high marks for comfort or safety, but it is economical.

Most buses make many stops along the way, and this, combined with low-horsepower engines, can make for very low average speeds. With its very high population densities, El Salvador often makes little distinction between urban and rural bus services. Buses can be flagged almost anywhere along highways and rural roads. Express buses operate only on a handful of routes, in particular on routes radiating from San Salvador to Santa Ana, Sonsonate and San Miguel. Although faster, they are nearly as uncomfortable as regular buses.

One particularity of bus service in El Salvador is that nearly all intercity and rural routes are numbered, with route numbers and destinations painted right onto the bus. Routes in the central part of the country are numbered in the 100s, routes in the west in the 200s, those in the east in the 300s, and some regional or rural routes in the 400s and 500s. Some route numbers will be provided here in the chapters dealing with each region.

Terminals

In the big cities and larger towns, buses operate from reasonably well organized terminals. Things usually are not as chaotic as they sometimes appear to foreigners. In San Salvador, there are four main terminals — the eastern, western, southern and international terminals, depending on destination. They are scattered across different parts of the city. More information is given in the San Salvador section. In the smaller towns, buses tend to stop in unsheltered and unmarked spots near the public market or the central plaza. In a few instances they merely pass by along the highway.

Schedules

When going to a small town that is any distance from where you are staying, it is best to get an early start unless you plan to spend the night there. From some towns, the last bus out goes in the early or middle afternoon. Even on heavily travelled routes, service ends shortly after dusk. Most Salvadorans are early risers, and visitors should consider following their example while in the country.

On any of the busier routes, service is so frequent that there is little need to inquire ahead about schedules. Travellers need merely go to the terminal, and the wait is not likely to be more than a few minutes. The same applies to flagging buses along a busy highway. Even many of the secondary intercity links are served two or three times an hour. When going to a remote area or a small village, however, it can be useful to inquire in advance. Usually the only way to get reliable information is to go to the terminal from which you expect to leave and ask around as best you can. There are no printed timetables, and even if you can get through by telephone, there is no assurance that the person who answers will have the information you are looking for.

For information on bus travel to other Central American countries, see page 30.

■ Trains and Airplanes

All passenger train service in El Salvador was halted in the early 1980s because of the risk of derailments caused by rebel sabotage. Freight trains continued operating throughout the war, but crew members rode in armoured or sandbagged compartments. Some very limited passenger service has been restored in the western part of the country. See page 102.

Light aircraft provide regular passenger service between San Salvador, San Miguel and other points in the eastern part of the country. See page 122.

■ Hitchhiking

Hitchhiking is not widely practised and should not really be attempted except in some remote villages where there is little alternative.

Money and Banking

The Salvadoran currency is the **colón**, named for Cristóbal Colón, known in English as Christopher Columbus. There are banknotes for 100, 50, 25, 10 and 5 colones, and coins for one colón and for 50, 25, 10 and 5 centavos. The 50-centavo coins are not very common. Some of the older coins are quite large and heavy. A new issue of smaller, lighter coins was introduced in the 1980s. The new and old coins circulate together, and visitors may find this perplexing at first.

The colón is represented by the letter C with a stroke through it, similar to the cent sign used in the United States and Canada. Thus ¢25 indicates 25 colones.

Prices in this guide are shown in United States dollars. There are two reasons for this. The first is that many readers are already familiar with the U.S. dollar and have a good grasp of the value of something expressed in this currency. The second reason is that prices expressed in dollars have remained more constant over the years than prices expressed in colones. Inflation has been balanced by devaluations. **Though prices are shown here in dollars, most things must be paid for in colones.**

■ Exchanging Money

As of late 1994, the U.S. dollar was worth 8.75 colones at the official exchange rate. This is the rate used for currency transactions between banks. Spreads between buying and selling rates have been quite narrow in recent times, usually below 1.5 per cent.

During the 1980s, exchange controls led to a flourishing black market for U.S. dollars. This is no longer the case. Visitors should give wide berth to anyone who purports to offer higher rates. Colones, by the way, can be changed back to dollars at the end of a visit. This should be done before leaving El Salvador since they fetch very poor rates elsewhere.

Canadians and Europeans bound for El Salvador are strongly urged to take most of their money in U.S. dollars, in cash or travellers' cheques or both. Canadian and European currencies are nearly impossible to exchange in El Salvador. People from other parts of the world are already well accustomed to the idea of travelling with U.S. dollars and do not need reminding of the importance of this.

U.S. currency can be changed to colones at most bank branches in El Salvador and at all currency dealers. Currency dealers (known in Spanish as *casas de cambio*) tend to stay open longer hours and provide faster service than banks, and they offer similar exchange rates. Some hotels also exchange dollars, but rates are usually poor. Bank hours vary, though most branches are shut by mid-afternoon. The banks have branches in all cities and larger towns, whereas the *casas de cambio* have nearly all their branches in the big cities.

Should it become necessary to exchange a currency other than the U.S. dollar or one of the Central American currencies, the place to go is El Salvador's central bank, Banco Central de Reserva, Centro de Gobierno, Avenida Juan Pablo II, San Salvador.

In the smaller towns — and anywhere at all on weekends — it can be harder to change money. Even in San Salvador only a handful of banks and *casas de cambio* are open Saturdays and, at last word, none on Sundays or holidays. The obvious advice, then, is to change money in one of the bigger cities and to do it on weekdays. There is a currency exchange office at the international airport, but it is not open at night. For visitors who are stuck without colones, taxi drivers at the airport will accept U.S. dollars, and small amounts can be exchanged upon arrival at the hotel. Those who arrive by land will find freelance currency dealers at the border waving large wads of cash. It is a good idea to change only small amounts because their rates are sometimes poor.

■ **Exchange Rates**

Here are some exchange rates valid in October 1994, based on a rate of 8.70 colones to the U.S. dollar, which was the average paid by banks and *casas de cambio*:

- 1 **$US** = 8.70 colones
  1 colón = 11.5 U.S. cents
- 1 **$Cdn** = 6.45 colones
  1 colón = 15.5 Canadian cents
- 1 **FF** = 1.51 colones
  1 colón = 66 French centimes
- 1 **£** = 13.75 colones
  1 colón = 7.3 British pence
- 1 **German mark** = 5.64 colones
  1 colón = 17.8 German pfennigs

■ **Travellers' Cheques**

Travellers' cheques are more difficult to exchange than cash. Some *casas de cambio* that used to accept them no longer do so. At the time of writing, **Banco Agrícola Comercial** was the most helpful financial institution when it came to travellers' cheques. As well as the cheques themselves, they require the sales receipt, a document that normally should be kept separate. Despite the inconvenience, it is probably a good idea, for reasons of security, to carry some U.S. travellers' cheques as well as U.S. cash. And it is preferable for the cash to be in a mixture of large and small denominations. The smaller bills can come in handy at the beginning or end of a trip.

■ **Credit Cards**

Credit cards can also come in handy. They are accepted by many hotels and by some restaurants and shops. They can also be used to pay for car rentals or airline tickets. Visa and Mastercard are the most widely accepted, followed by American Express. Diners Club cards are also honoured in some spots. This guidebook indicates which hotels accept credit cards. The abbreviations used are VI for Visa, MC for Mastercard, AE for American Express and DC for Diners Club.

These same cards can come to the rescue of travellers who run short of cash. Bank branches do not provide cash advances as they do in many countries, but this service is offered during normal office hours by the central office of **Credomatic**, which coordinates **Visa** and **Mastercard** transactions for Salvadoran banks. It is essential to bring your passport as well as your credit card. **American Express** and **Diners Club** cardholders should check before leaving home about arrangements for obtaining cash advances or transfers in El Salvador. They all have offices in San Salvador.

Credomatic (for Visa or Mastercard)
55ª Avenida Sur between Alameda Roosevelt and Avenida Olímpica,
☎ 224-5155, 224-5100 or 224-5257.

American Express
Centro Comercial Mascota,
km 4½, Carretera a Santa Tecla,
☎ 279-3844.

Diners Club
67ª Avenida Norte #100,
Colonia Escalón,
☎ 224-6349, 224-6251 or 223-2888.

■ **Sending Money**

Should it become necessary to have money sent from home, banks can handle this by telegraphic transfer, but a faster, cheaper and more reliable way to transfer funds is to have the money deposited into a credit card account and then withdraw it in the form of a cash advance.

■ **Taxes and Tipping**

Value-Added Tax

Most goods and services in El Salvador are subject to a value-added tax which, at the time of writing, stands at 10 per cent. It is easy not to notice this tax because most of the time it is already included in the price. When you buy something at a shop or eat at a restaurant, the amount that appears on the price tag or the menu is the price you pay, and it includes the tax.

There are some exceptions to this. Lower- and medium-priced hotels nearly always include the tax in the rates they present to the public, but most upper-range hotels add it on top, which can sometimes make for an unpleasant surprise when you receive your bill. We find this practice deceitful, even if it is common in many countries. **All hotel prices we show in this book have the tax already added.**

Taxes on Air Travel

International airline tickets purchased in El Salvador are subject to a tax of 10 per cent, which applies on top of the published fare. All air travellers must pay a departure tax of $17 when checking in for international flights, regardless of where the tickets were purchased. This may be paid in U.S. dollars or in colones. It can be a useful way to get rid of any unspent Salvadoran currency before leaving the country.

Tipping

Taxi drivers do not expect to be tipped, but if they help you with baggage or take you to a remote or hard-to-find spot, a tip will be highly appreciated. Porters should be tipped according to the volume of baggage and the distance they carry it, but usually no more than $2 unless your baggage is quite voluminous or something heavy has to be hauled up steps. Chambermaids are poorly paid and can put tips to good use.

Waiters at bars and restaurants should get tips equal to about 10 per cent of the bill, but offer more if the bill is for a small amount, or if the service has been especially good, or if you are charging the tip to a credit card (in which case management may retain part of it).

Language

Spanish is the sole official language of El Salvador and is spoken everywhere. In a few villages and small towns, Nahua is also spoken by some Indian people. English is spoken at some hotels and restaurants, by some members of the country's educated elite, and by emigrants who have returned from the United States.

Anyone who steps outside the cocoon of a tour group or resort hotel will almost certainly be thrust into situations where a knowledge of Spanish is useful. That does not mean they will be totally lost if they do not speak Spanish. What it does mean is that they will have to show patience, grace, good humour and the odd bit of ingenuity. Sign language combined with a few key words is often useful, and having pen and paper at the ready can help in some situations. A complete glossary is provided in the last pages of this book. As well, a pocket dictionary can be useful for signs or menus, and it many not hurt to spend a couple of hours with a phrase book trying to memorize a few lines.

■ Pronunciation

In a few places in this book, pronunciations of some difficult words or names are shown phonetically, with accented syllables in upper case. "A" is pronounced as in cat, "ay" rhymes with day, "ee" rhymes with see, "oo" rhymes with too, and "ow" rhymes with cow. The "ah" sound does not exist in Spanish; some people imagine, mistakenly, that it makes them sound erudite. The letter "j" (as well as "g" when followed by an "e" or "i") has a guttural sound not found in English; "kh" will be used here to show that sound.

Mail and Telecommunications

■ Mail

Postal service in El Salvador is exceedingly slow. Both inbound and outbound letters can take many weeks to reach their destinations.

■ Telephone

Telephone service is provided by a government-owned company called **Antel**, which operates telephone centres for local and long-distance calls throughout the country, including most small towns. Hours of operation vary. To place a call at an Antel office, it is necessary to give a clerk the number being called and to leave a deposit. When a line is free, sometimes after a long wait, the caller will be directed to one of several telephone booths along the wall, which are identified by number. Accounts are settled after the call is completed.

Rates within El Salvador are very cheap, usually just a few pennies even for a long-distance call. International rates, on the other hand, are steep, running at more than $2 a minute to the United States, with a three-minute minimum, and much higher to most other countries. Rates are especially high to Canada, which Antel has decreed is part of Europe! When calling Canada or Europe, it is often much cheaper to call collect. Telephone subscribers in the United States have the option of using **Call Direct** service, with calls routed through a U.S. operator. From most telephones in El Salvador, the numbers to call are 190 for AT&T, 191 for Sprint and 195 for MCI. A similar service was expected to be in place for Canadians by early 1995.

International calls placed from hotels often entail hefty surcharges. Before calling, it is best to check with the hotel operator to see how high the charge will be.

There are very few public telephones in El Salvador. Some of them accept only the older, larger coins. It is easy to dial long-distance calls within El Salvador, but international calls can be placed only through the operator, with the charges reversed. Dial 113.

All telephone numbers have seven digits. The switch over from six-digit numbers took place in October 1994, and many signs and printed items continue to show the old six-digit numbers. To convert a six-digit number to the new seven-digit number, simply place the appropriate digit in front. All regular numbers in San Salvador begin with 2, those elsewhere in the central part of the country with 3, those in the west with 4, and those in the east with 6. These do not constitute area codes or city codes: local and long-distance calls are dialled the same way.

The international telephone code for El Salvador is 503. To call El Salvador from abroad, first enter the international access code, then 503, then the seven-digit local number.

Fax machines have come into common use in El Salvador. Most of the larger hotels can provide fax service for their guests. Some Antel offices also provide fax service.

Accommodation

Because of the 12-year hiatus that El Salvador's tourism industry had to observe while the nasty business of a civil war was conducted, facilities in many parts of the country are rather limited. This is not the case in San Salvador, which has several five-star hotels and a broad choice of hotels in other categories. There are also good hotels at certain beach resorts and pleasant, if not luxurious, places to stay in a few of the smaller towns.

Even in San Salvador, however, a surge of business travel has meant that space is sometimes scarce at the more expensive hotels. And in several towns the lodging situation is downright dismal, with only the most basic sorts of hotels available — not a great hardship, perhaps, for budget travellers who prefer not to spend very much anyway, but it can be a deterrent for visitors who seek greater levels of comfort or charm.

■ Hotels

There are reasonable choices of accommodation in every region of the country if not in every town. For example, the city of Sonsonate, in the southwestern part of the country, is singularly bereft of pleasant places to stay, but in the small town of Apaneca to its northwest there is a lovely mountain inn. San Miguel, in eastern El Salvador, has several decent hotels at varied prices, but in most other parts of the region lodgings tend to be rudimentary, with the exception of a couple of beach hotels.

In choosing hotels that appear in this guidebook, we have looked for places in varied price categories that offer reasonable levels of appeal, good standards of cleanliness, and useful locations. We have not attempted to provide comprehensive lists, preferring to take a more selective approach. Prices that appear here are for double occupancy (in a few instances, prices for single occupancy are also shown where there is a sizable gap). These prices include taxes and were valid at the time each establishment was visited. Needless to say, they are subject to change.

Many hotels and *hospedajes*, in big towns and small, have been left out because often they are places where not many foreign visitors would choose voluntarily to stay. This does not mean that travellers who want to stay overnight in a town for which we provide no hotel listing should immediately give up on the idea, but it does mean they may have to settle for something rather primitive.

■ *Hospedajes*

The term *hospedaje* is often used to designate a modest and very simple hotel. There is nothing pejorative about the term, and some *hospedajes* are reasonably pleasant, but many really are quite bleak. In certain towns it would be nice to have a choice extending beyond what this term applies. A few of the better ones will be mentioned in this guidebook.

■ Camping

Formal campgrounds are virtually unknown in El Salvador, although there are a few places where camping is possible, including certain *turicentros*. The same applies to trailer parks. Campers should be warned that the crime problem in some parts of the country leaves them somewhat vulnerable.

Restaurants

Dining out is one of the pleasures of travel, and El Salvador is no exception. The country has many restaurants where visitors can eat very well indeed. It would be an exaggeration, however, to say that El Salvador is a place people visit specifically because of the food. As good as the food often is, menus even at some of the better restaurants tend to lack originality, sticking mostly to tried-and-true steak or shrimp dishes. Still, there are enough good spots around that the intrepid gourmet will not leave disappointed.

San Salvador, which is home to most of the country's wealthy families and the main base for most business travellers, has by far the biggest selection of fine restaurants. Steak eaters will come away especially happy, although lovers of fish, seafood and pasta will not be disappointed either. Mexican, Spanish, Argentinean and Chinese restaurants help round out the selection.

In the smaller towns and beach resorts, the selection is more limited. At La Libertad, on the coast near San Salvador, beaches and hotels have many deficiencies, but the food is very good and several restaurants are quite pleasant. Along the Costa del Sol, the hotels do a reasonable job of keeping visitors decently fed. In the eastern part of the country, several restaurants offer special versions of *mariscada*, a seafood dish. Several beaches, notably Playa El Cuco south of San Miguel, have humble restaurants offering tasty fresh fish and seafood in modest surroundings and at modest prices. Further from the coast, meat tends to dominate most menus.

Throughout the country there exist countless small restaurants and *comedores* offering ordinary fare at very reasonable prices. The *plato típico* (typical meal) often consists of a small piece of steak accompanied by black beans, soft white cheese and fried bananas. In some places visitors are expected to walk right into the kitchen and point to what they want from the pots boiling on the stove. When a sign outside a restaurant refers to *comida a la vista*, that means the meals of the day are out on display. At many public markets there are stalls offering meals, often with long benches and tables where customers eat communally.

A very popular fast food is the *pupusa* (see above). Another is southern-style fried chicken, often confined to modern, air-conditioned establishments in the larger towns and cities. Colonel Sanders has not arrived in El Salvador, having been pre-empted by the Guatemalan-based *Pollo Campero* chain, which has a powerful presence. Other fried chicken chains include *Pollo Indio* and *Pollo Campestre*. Pizza is also popular among city dwellers. Both *Pizza Hut* and *Toto's*, a local chain, are highly visible, as are several internationally known hamburger chains. For desert, the Costa Rican-based *Pops* and Mexican-based *Holanda* ice cream chains both offer wide selections of flavours. Some of the tropical fruit sorbets are especially nice.

Soft drinks, both the familiar international brands and local brands, are readily available. In some places tinned fruit drinks are also offered. Beer is by far the most popular alcoholic drink. The two best-selling brands are

> ### Salvadoran Cuisine
>
> The favourite fast food in El Salvador, and the true national dish, is the pupusa, a cornmeal tortilla cooked on a griddle and stuffed with cheese, black beans or other fillings that can include ground beef or chicharrón, deep-fried pork rinds. Pupusas are usually accompanied on the side by spicy pickled cabbage. They do not appear very often on the menus of ordinary restaurants, but there are found just about everywhere else. Many street stalls and specialized restaurants and shops called pupusarías serve them hot off the griddle, and many people also prepare them at home. When prepared without a meat filling, pupusas are a vegetarian's dream come true.
>
> A mariscada is altogether a different kettle of fish. It is a cross between a soup and stew loaded with fresh seafood, and it is one of El Salvador's great culinary delights. Only a handful of restaurants offer the classic mariscada (a few others use the term to designate an ordinary seafood platter), and they are mostly in the eastern part of the country. The basic recipe calls for lobster, crab, shrimp, fish and other fresh ingredients (such as oysters in some instances) cooked in a special broth. Each restaurant offering mariscada has developed its own variation, and these recipes are guarded with great secrecy.

Pilsener, which has an ace of hearts on the label, and the higher-priced *Suprema*. Both are watery, American-style lagers, but in hot weather they go down easily, and they are inexpensive.

The more expensive restaurants offer selections of wines, with an emphasis on Spanish and Chilean vintages. Wine prices are fairly high, as are the prices of liquor imported from outside Central America. Botrán rum from Guatemala is inexpensive and of good quality. The most popular of Salvadoran liquors is something called *Tic-Tack*. This is a brand of *aguardiente*, which is unmatured sugar-cane liquor. It is sold very cheaply at liquor stores and low-life bars.

Entertainment

Poverty and fear of crime have combined to restrict offerings in the area of entertainment, especially outside San Salvador.

In the larger cities cinemas offer a selection of American films plus the occasional Latin American or European offering. Most of the higher-brow American films are subtitled rather than dubbed in Spanish, leaving them accessible to English-speakers.

Several open-air night clubs in San Salvador present salsa or rock bands, especially on weekends. They offer a lively scene, with plenty of dancing.

Saints' Days

In the smaller cities and towns, the entertainment scene is severely limited. An exception occurs during the annual festival in each town, when there are masked processions, often with elaborate costumes.

The festivities sometimes go on for several days, and at most times of the year there is a festival taking place in some town or other. A comprehensive list, titled *Calendario de Fiestas Patronales de El Salvador*, is available from the tourism office in San Salvador (*Calle Rubén Darío 619*).

There is no guarantee that visitors who arrive in a particular town during festival period will find much going on, and not every town puts on much of a show. In some cases it amounts to a humble religious procession and little more. But in other towns the local people go all out to have fun.

Generally speaking, medium-sized towns are the places where the festivals are most enjoyable. They are big enough to draw a good crowd and yet small enough to maintain a level of intimacy. In cases where the celebration lasts many days, festivities tend to be concentrated at the beginning and the end. In every instance the times of parades and other events can vary.

Fútbol

Lovers of soccer (known as football everywhere outside North America) should have a better time of it. *El fútbol* is practically the national religion, and there is scarcely a village in the country without a heavily used playing field. For the dates and times of professional matches, check local newspapers or, better still, ask a taxi driver or male hotel clerk when his favourite team is playing. Tickets are inexpensive, so try for the better seats.

Shopping

A favourite class of items for shoppers visiting from abroad are the towels, bathrobes and other textile creations bearing the brightly coloured impressions of rural life developed in the small town of La Palma in the north of the country. They make good gifts, they are easy to pack, and they are distinctively Salvadoran.

The designs from La Palma have also made their way onto a prodigious variety of carved wooden objects, jewellery boxes, ceramics, leather goods and other items. They are bright and cheerful, and again they are distinctive. Several other towns are noted for handicrafts production, including Ilobasco for its hand-painted ceramics, Nahuizalco for its elaborate wicker creations, and Chalchuapa for its masks. Stuffed toys, particularly in the shape of brightly coloured parakeets and other tropical birds, are also popular items.

Visitors should take the opportunity to visit the towns where some of these crafts are produced, but even if they cannot, there are excellent selections at two of the public markets in San Salvador (see page 78). A knack for bargaining is required to get the best prices. Buying several items from the same market stall increases the chance of getting a discount. There are also many shops, which provide air conditioning but no bargaining and somewhat higher prices.

Shopping opportunities are more limited in the smaller towns, except for those where some of the items are produced. For items of practical day-to-day use, public markets, city-centre shopping areas and suburban shopping centres can satisfy most needs.

Press and Broadcasting

There are four daily newspapers in El Salvador, all in Spanish and all published in the capital. *La Prensa Gráfica* provides the most complete information and is generally quite conservative in outlook. *El Diario de Hoy* has a noticeable right-wing slant and devotes many pages to the comings and goings of people in high society. Two smaller papers, *Diario Latino* and *El Mundo* (the latter an afternoon paper) are seen as somewhat more liberal. It is hard to find foreign newspapers, though the *Miami Herald* is sold at a couple of the bigger hotels.

El Salvador has six television stations, all in Spanish, which can be picked up anywhere in the country. A handful of hotels offer cable or satellite television with some stations from the U.S. Radio is highly commercial, but in San Salvador there are a couple of interesting stations on the FM band. Travellers who are keen on keeping abreast of world events should consider bringing a small short-wave radio.

Miscellaneous

■ **Business Hours and Holidays**

Hours

Office hours in El Salvador are comparable to those in North America, with most offices opening between 8 a.m. and 9 a.m. and closing between 4 p.m. and 5 p.m., with a one-hour lunch break around noon. Many Salvadorans tend to be more casual than people from northern latitudes in matters of punctuality, and meetings often start late. It is always a good idea to bring reading material.

Holidays

Official holidays are:
January 1: New Year's Day
Floating dates: Easter Sunday and the three days preceding it
May 1: Labour Day
August 3-6: *El Salvador del Mundo* (The Saviour of the World), observed more in San Salvador than in the rest of the country
September 15: Independence Day
December 25: Christmas Day

Other holidays are observed unofficially. These include:
October 12: *Día de la Raza* (Day of the Race)
November 2: *Día de los Muertos* (Day of the Dead).

Special Events

Things tend to shut down in San Salvador for the entire first week of August, for the *El Divino Salvador del Mundo* festival. Easter is a very important celebration, and there are many processions during Holy Week, the period leading up to Easter. The city of Sonsonate in the western part of the country is noted for its Holy Week processions.

Almost every town and village in El Salvador has a saint's day or festival that is marked by celebrations of some sort, often including religious processions or secular parades with brightly coloured costumes and masks. These are scattered throughout the year.

■ **Time Zones**

El Salvador stays on Central Standard Time year-round. This is one hour behind Eastern Standard Time in North America and two hours behind Eastern Daylight Time (in summer). Expressed another way, it is one hour ahead of Pacific Daylight Time and two hours ahead of Pacific Standard Time. It is also six hours behind Greenwich Mean Time, seven hours behind Winter Time in most of western Europe, and eight hours behind European Summer Time.

■ **Weights and Measures**

El Salvador uses a mixture of metric and American measures. Distances are normally expressed in metres (abbreviated simply as m) and kilometres (km). Food is often sold by the pound (*libra*), while gasoline is sold by the U.S. gallon (*galón*). Temperatures are given in degrees Celsius (sometimes called Centigrade).

British gallon = 4.55 l
US gallon = 3.79 l
1 mi = 1.6 km
1 km = 0.62 mi
1 ft. = 30 cm

■ **Electricity**

For electrical appliances, El Salvador uses the 60-cycle, 110-volt system, the same as in North America. Appliances sold in North America can be used without voltage converters. Most wall outlets take only the old-style two flat-pronged plugs, however. Anything with three-pronged plugs may require a plug adaptor, available at hardware stores. European appliances require voltage converters **and** plug adaptors.

OUTDOOR ACTIVITIES

From its beaches to its volcanoes to its nature reserves, El Salvador offers activities to satisfy the yearnings of many visitors. Outdoor activities are outlined in the chapters covering each region of the country, but here is a brief summary of what to expect.

Beaches and Swimming

El Salvador has a long coastline on the Pacific. Many beaches remain close to their original state and are virtually untouched, but some others have been developed to receive visitors. Most beaches have strong undertows, and swimmers should be cautious. A notable exception is **Playa El Tamarindo**, with its dark volcanic sand, facing the calm Gulf of Fonseca. There are several other beaches nearby, including tiny **Playa Torola** in a partly sheltered bay. Perhaps the best beaches are those along the **Costa del Sol**, with expanses of pale sand and moderate surf.

El Salvador also offers opportunities for lake swimming, notably in easy-to-reach **Lago de Coatepeque** in the west of the country, **Lago de Ilopango** in the centre and **Laguna Apastepeque** further east. Perhaps more enticing are the harder-to-reach **Lago de Güija**, which straddles the border with Guatemala, and **Laguna de Alegría**, high in the mountains near the town of Berlín and fed by both hot and cold springs. In the north, near the town of La Palma, the icy **Río Nunuapa** is suitable for swimming.

52 Outdoor Activities

Virtually all the government-run *turicentros* offer outdoor pools. The most spectacular is **Los Chorros**, a short distance outside San Salvador, where a series of magnificent natural pools and cascades are surrounded by high ridges and tropical vegetation.

Surfing

The high waves which may create a hazard for swimmers are a delight for surfers, and El Salvador has several beaches with excellent surfing opportunities. The most noted of them is **Playa El Sunzal**, an undeveloped beach just west of the resort town of La Libertad.

Boating

Boating is not highly developed as a leisure activity in El Salvador, but there are several opportunities for short cruises, notably in the estuaries near the **Costa del Sol** and **Barra de Santiago** with their abundant bird life. Fishermen can also take visitors out to see the surroundings of **Lago de Güija** and birdlife along **Laguna de Jocotal**.

Nature Reserves

Parque Nacional de Montecristo, where El Salvador converges with Guatemala and Honduras, is one of the few breeding grounds left for the quetzal, that most revered of Central American birds. Outside the breeding season, visitors can see the fascinating and little developed mountain park that contains El Salvador's only remaining cloud forest. Parts of the park are accessible year-round. It also has a wide variety of orchids.

Laguna de Jocotal, along the coastal plain near Usulután, lies in a semi-protected area with an abundance of bird life.

Hiking

El Salvador's many volcanoes provide wonderful opportunities for hikers. In the western part of the country, the heavily vegetated **Santa Ana** volcano and the more slippery Izalco volcano (it erupted as recently as 1957, and its slopes remain covered with bare lava) provide interesting challenges. In the east, hikers can attack the **Conchagua** volcano and the **San Miguel** volcano, also known as **Chaparrastique**, where it is possible to descend deep inside the cone. Closer to San Salvador, the **San Salvador** and **Guazapa** volcanoes are popular spots for hikers.

In the north of the country, hikers can ascend the non-volcanic **Montecristo**, inside the national park and nature reserve of the same name, and **Cerro El Pital**, at 2,730 m (8,960 ft) the highest peak in El Salvador. In the west, near the town of Apaneca, a gentle track leads 8 km (5 mi) to **Laguna Verde**.

Bicycling

Bicycling is a means of transport for some Salvadorans, especially in rural areas, but few think of it as a leisure activity. The country is richly endowed with paved, lightly travelled secondary highways that pass through gorgeous hilly countryside — rather challenging for novices but highly rewarding for more experienced cyclists. A few routes are suggested in the chapters covering different regions of the country.

Foreigners riding bicycles in El Salvador are seen as something of an oddity, and indeed they are very rare, but they are well accommodated. Some intercity and rural buses have baggage racks on the roof that will take bicycles for a small supplement to the fare. Cyclists may be wise, however, to avoid more remote stretches of road because of the threat of banditry. Before setting out, it is a good idea to inquire locally about the safety of a planned route. Cycling also is not really advisable in San Salvador because of heavy motor traffic and horrendous pollution. Local cyclists commonly wear protective masks over the mouth and nose.

Tennis and Golf

These are both considered elite pursuits in El Salvador and are not high developed. Some of the bigger hotels in San Salvador can arrange access to tennis courts or to a nine-hole golf course.

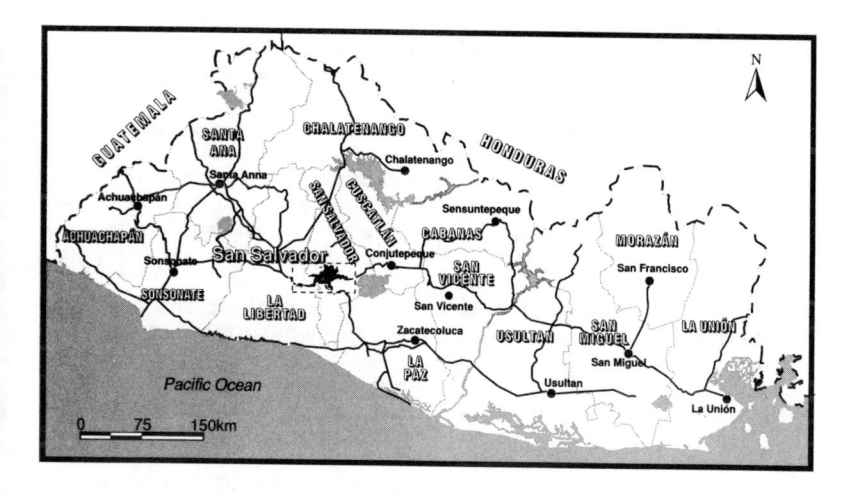

SAN SALVADOR

Many visitors will catch their first glimpse of El Salvador in the country's capital. This seems a pity for, despite the city's impressive natural setting, the beauty and charm that draw visitors to many parts of the country are largely absent in San Salvador itself. This is a big, bustling and, at times, intimidating place, and not everyone will warm to it. That said, it does offer many comforts and conveniences, and some areas are attractive. The city is set in a natural bowl, with high hills to the north and west. The sight of the San Salvador volcano looming in the distance adds character to the place. With its numerous hotels and restaurants, the city is an excellent base for excursions to many parts of the country.

Alas, the traditional city centre is essentially a disaster. San Salvador was a backwater during the colonial era and achieved real importance only in the 19th century. In more recent times, the wealthy have firmly turned their backs on the city centre and concentrated their spending and investment in the hilly districts to the west and southwest. The result is a downtown area that has been abandoned to the poor and shows the sort of blight that has wounded all too many cities in the United States. Important public buildings and once proud civic plazas lie neglected.

The modern Roman Catholic cathedral is a giant concrete shell that for decades has remained in an ugly, unfinished state. The National Palace was heavily damaged in the 1986 earthquake and is only slowly being restored. Other buildings are simply being left to crumble. The streets of the centre pullulate throughout the day with informal commerce as vendors set up simple stalls to display their often meagre wares. Sidewalks along several streets are almost impassable, and the air is fouled by acrid clouds of bus exhaust. At night the city centre is the domain of thieves and muggers.

The area east of the centre is poor and depressed. Up the hill at the other end of the city, and at the other end of the social scale, is Colonia Escalón, with swank restaurants and boutiques and luxurious residences surrounded by high walls. Colonia San Benito, to the southwest, is another well-to-do area, which includes the *zona rosa* with many restaurants, bars and fancy shops. Santa Anita, further southwest, is beginning to emerge. Almost every city in the world has its share of segregation between rich and poor, but in San Salvador it is really very stark. In several areas around the outskirts, rural migrants have built crude dwellings on hillsides and ravines. Construction materials in some cases consist of little more than cardboard and plastic sheeting.

San Salvador and its outlying areas are home to nearly one-quarter of El Salvador's six million people, who have shown remarkable energy and cheerfulness under very trying circumstances. With the end of the civil war, there has been a construction boom, but this has been most evident in the wealthier areas. Still, new factories are popping up here and there around the outskirts, promising steady employment to a growing number of people, and many will be able to improve their standards of living.

Conventional tourist attractions do not abound in San Salvador. The old city centre, despite its decrepitude, is worth a visit and a short stroll. The museum scene is dead: the Museo Nacional, which displayed archeological items, has closed because of structural weaknesses in the building housing it, and no new site has been found yet. There is no art museum, but there are one or two galleries to see.

Several areas of the city are worth taking note of for their restaurants or their shopping, and there are two big markets with handicrafts items. Those interested in Salvadoran history or politics may want to visit the chapel where Archbishop Oscar Romero was assassinated in 1980. There are several parks to see, especially Parque Balboa in the south of the city, with a mountain lookout called La Puerta del Diablo.

A little further south is the charming old village of Panchimalco. Other points just outside the city include Los Chorros, a series of natural pools in a stunning tropical setting, and Lago de Ilopango, a big lake in a scenic mountain location. Hikers can climb the San Salvador volcano.

Two days should be more than sufficient to see San Salvador and its surroundings, but many visitors will choose to stay longer, using the city as a base from which to visit some of the many points in the central or western parts of the country that can be seen on an easy day's excursion from the capital. These areas are covered in the following chapters.

Finding Your Way Around

■ **General Orientation**

The layout of San Salvador is not especially complicated. In much of the city, the streets form a rectangular grid pattern, and many streets have numbers instead of names, making them easier to find. The traditional city centre has fallen into a state of decrepitude and lost much of its earlier importance, but it still lies at the core of the street numbering system. The unfinished and unsightly metropolitan cathedral has a large dome that can be used as a reference point in this part of the city. One corner of the block it occupies marks the point from which all street numbers rise.

There is no "zero" street or avenue. From the intersection near the cathedral, Calle Arce runs west, Calle Delgado runs east, Avenida España runs north and Avenida Cuscatlán runs south. Most other streets and avenues in the central area and in some districts beyond are numbered, and the numbers reflect the distance from this point. Streets run east and west, avenues north and south. Even-numbered avenues lie to the east and odd-numbered avenues to the north, while even-numbered streets lie to the south and odd-numbered streets to the north. Many addresses have a cardinal point of the compass attached to them — *poniente* for west, *oriente* for east, *norte* for north and *sur* for south — reflecting their relation to one of these dividing lines. To the west, Alameda Roosevelt and then Paseo Escalón form the dividing line between north and south.

The city sprawls in all directions, but this sprawl is uneven, in part because topography gets in the way and in part because the wealthy chose to build their houses and, later, their businesses on higher ground to the west. Thus the western part of the city is more developed than the east. The street numbering system breaks down in many areas where hills or gulleys interfere or where new residential areas are laid out with little reference to their surroundings.

Perhaps the single most important street in the city is known as Paseo Escalón in the west, changing names to Alameda Roosevelt further east and later to Calle Rubén Darío in the city centre. Rubén Darío becomes a one-way street, carrying eastbound traffic, while Calle Arce, one block north, carries westbound traffic. Several blocks further north is Alameda Juan Pablo II, named after a famous Polish pope. This street runs past the Centro de Gobierno, or government centre, a cluster of buildings which house many government ministries and agencies. It changes names to Boulevard Ejército Nacional in the east and to Calle San Antonio Abad in the west.

Another important artery is Boulevard Los Héroes, running southwest from the campus of the Universidad National de El Salvador, past the Hotel Camino Real and the Metrocentro and Metrosur shopping centres, changing names to 49ª Avenida, heading south past a big soccer stadium, the fairgrounds and the handicrafts market, running eventually into the Autopista Sur, a four-lane highway which goes to the international airport about 40 km (25 mi) south of the city. A smaller airport, used for domestic and military flights, is situated in Ilopango on the eastern outskirts of the city.

San Salvador

By Bus

A great profusion of buses serves all parts of the city. Regular buses are painted blue and white and, at the time of writing, charge a fare of 80 centavos, equal to about 9 U.S. cents. *Preferencial* buses painted red and white operate on many of the same routes, tend to be somewhat less cramped, and charge 1.25 colones, equal to about 14 U.S. cents. These amounts may seem trivial, but to many bus users they represent real money.

Buses run very frequently on key routes, but even so they are often overcrowded. It is not a good idea to try carrying large pieces of baggage aboard. There are no maps indicating which bus routes go where, and most bus stops are unmarked. To get almost anywhere, visitors will have to ask directions, a real challenge for those whose Spanish is deficient. Anyone who expects to be using city buses should seek guidance from hotel staff or from the tourism office, Calle Rubén Darío 619. Service on most routes ends by 9 p.m.

Intercity Buses

Intercity and rural buses operate from four terminals in San Salvador. Three terminals serve points within El Salvador and provide scarcely any comfort or amenities, while the fourth, known as **Puerto Bus** (☎ 222-2158), serves international routes. Puerto Bus, situated on Alameda Juan Pablo II at 19ª Avenida Norte near the Centro de Gobierno, has shops and restaurants as well as a spacious ticketing area and comfortable waiting rooms. There are more than 20 buses a day to Guatemala City and two or three to Tegucigalpa, in Honduras. Luxury bus service to these same points is provided by **King Quality** (☎ 222-3224 or 279-4166), which uses the Hotel Presidente in Colonia San Benito as its terminal. To Managua, Nicaragua, **Tica-Bus** (☎ 222-4808) has daily direct service, using the humble Hotel San Carlos, Calle Concepción 121, as its terminal. See page 30 for further information on these services.

Buses to the western part of the country and to some points along the coast leave from the **Terminal de Occidente** (western terminal), situated southwest of the city centre near the intersection of Boulevard Venezuela and 49ª Avenida Sur. It is served by taxis and by city bus routes 4, 27 and 34. Buses from here include:

- 102 to La Libertad
- 108 to San Juan Opico, stopping at Joya de Cerén
- 201 to Santa Ana (those marked *Ordinario* also stop at Los Chorros, Ruinas de San Andrés, and El Congo for connections to Lago de Coatepeque and Cerro Verde)
- 202 to Santa Ana and Ahuachapán
- 205 to Sonsonate.

Buses heading southeast leave from the **Terminal del Sur** (southern terminal), sometimes known as the Terminal Rutas del Pacífico. It is located on the eastern side of the Autopista del Sur on the southern edge of the city and can be reached by taxi or by city bus route 11-B. Some buses make a loop through the south of the city before heading back to the highway and out into the countryside. Buses leaving from this terminal include:

- 133 to Zacatecoluca
- 134 to La Herradura, with connections to the Costa del Sol
- 495 direct to the Costa del Sol (infrequent service)

Buses to the eastern part of the country and some points in the centre and north leave from the **Terminal de Oriente** (eastern terminal), located in the east of the city in front of the railway freight sheds near where Avenida Juan Pablo II changes names to Boulevard Ejército Nacional. The closest cross street is 38ª Avenida Norte. The terminal can be reached by taxi or by city bus routes 7, 29, 33 or 34. Here is a partial list of intercity routes leaving from this terminal:

- 110 to San Sebastián
- 111 to Ilobasco
- 113 to Cojutepeque
- 116 to San Vicente
- 119 to La Palma and El Poy
- 125 to Chalatenango
- 301 to San Miguel
- 302 to Usulután
- 304 to La Unión
- 306 to Santa Rosa de Lima.

■ By Taxi

For many visitors, taxis are by far the most useful way of getting around the city, even though many of the vehicles are old and dilapidated. For most trips within the city, not counting the outlying districts, fares range between 15 and 30 colones ($1.75 to $3.50). Fares tend to rise after dark, and taxis parked in front of the big hotels often charge more than taxis that are flagged in the street.

Taxi meters are not used in El Salvador, and anyone who is concerned about being overcharged should ask about the fare before embarking. Between the city and the international airport the fixed rate is 125 colones, or a little under $15. Drivers do not expect tips, but those who help with baggage or who take passengers to a hard-to-find or out-of-the-way spots should get a little extra. For short trips around town, payment should be in colones only. For trips outside town, many drivers will accept U.S. dollars as well, although they are not obliged to.

Some visitors may want to consider using taxis for excursions outside the city. For half-day excursions this is usually cheaper than renting a car, and even for full-day excursions it may not cost that much more. It is essential to agree on a price beforehand and to make clear where you want to go and how much time you plan to spend in each place.

■ By Car

Although the rate of car ownership in El Salvador is very low, most cars are concentrated in San Salvador, and traffic congestion has grown much worse in recent years. There are few pieces of special advice to offer to motorists other than to avoid unfamiliar districts after dark. When parking in the city centre, motorists may be approached by children or even by adults offering to guard their vehicle. Usually they ask only for one or two colones, a very modest sum and a sensible precaution.

Highways radiate in several directions from San Salvador. For a brief outline, see page 35.

Car Rentals

Car rentals tend to cost slightly more in El Salvador than in North America, but prices can fluctuate. When checking prices, it is important to ask if taxes, insurance and mileage (or *kilometraje*) are included. Four-wheel-drive vehicles are sometimes available. Following is a list of car rental agencies and telephone numbers in San Salvador and at the international airport:

San Salvador

Avis: Airport (☎ 339-9268), Hotel Camino Real (☎ 223-9103), Hotel Presidente (☎ 279-4444, ext. 185), Hotel El Salvador (☎ 224-2710).
Budget: Airport (☎ 339-9186), 79ª Avenida Sur 6, Colonia La Mascota (☎ 279-2811 or 223-1668)
Hertz: Airport (☎ 339-9481), Calle Los Andes 16, Colonia Miramonte (☎ 226-8099), Hotel Presidente (☎ 279-4444, ext. 142)
Dollar: Prolongación Calle Arce 2226, between 41ª and 43ª Avenidas Norte (☎ 223-3108 or 279-2069)
Imosa: Calle Modelo 208, Barrio Candelaria (☎ 270-0950 or 270-0951)
Sure: Boulevard Los Héroes at 23ª Calle Poniente (☎ 225-1185 or 226-2982)
Superior: 3ª Calle Poniente at 15ª Avenida Norte (☎ 222-9111 or 222-2172)
Horus: Condominion Balam Quitze, Paseo Escalón (☎ 298-0500 or 298-5858)
Tropic: Avenida Olímpica 3597, Colonia Escalón (☎ 223-7947 or 279-3226)
Gigante: Boulevard Los Héroes north of the Hotel Camino Real (☎ 225-5624 or 225-6033)
Ocean: Centro Comercial Feria Rosa, Carretera a Santa Tecla (☎ 279-2174)
Renta Auto: 73ª Avenida Norte 330, Colonia Escalón (☎ 223-7397 or 224-1942)

■ **By Foot**

In many cities, walking around is the best way to see a place and to get the flavour of it. This is less true in San Salvador, where the city centre is rather decrepit and uninteresting. The sidewalks are narrow and are often commandeered by vendors who use the space for their stalls. Away from the city centre, sidewalks are often obstructed by parked cars. The disdain many motorists show toward pedestrians extends well beyond this; very few yield to pedestrians at intersections, and some crossings can be nightmarish. At night, pedestrians in many parts of the city are vulnerable to muggings or worse. This is not to suggest that visitors should avoid walking in San Salvador, but they should be aware that in many areas it can be less than pleasurable.

❓ Practical Information

■ **Tourist Information**

The *Instituto Salvadoreño de Turismo* (Mon-Fri 8 a.m. to 4 p.m., Calle Rubén Darío 619 between 9ª and 11ª Avenidas Sur, ☎ 222-8000 or 222-0960) can provide material in Spanish and English on tourist attractions as well as practical information on matters such as buses. They also provide crude mimeographed maps of the city and country, and can advise on organized weekend excursions to different parts of the country. Some staff members seem better informed than others. Besides this office in the centre of San Salvador, the *Instituto* has a counter at the international airport (open every day 8 a.m. to 5 p.m.). Hotel staff can often be helpful with practical information.

■ **Airports**

There are two airports near San Salvador. The **Aeropuerto Internacional de El Salvador** is situated about 40 km (25 mi) south of the city and is linked by a good four-lane highway. This airport handles all international flights. It has no regular bus service. The nearest town is Comalapa. Taxis between San Salvador and the airport charge about $15.

The old **Aeropuerto de Ilopango** on the eastern outskirts of San Salvador, just off the Carretera Panamericana, serves the tiny handful of domestic flights as well as military traffic. Taxi fare is about $8.

■ **Airline Offices**

Following are the addresses of city ticket offices and phone numbers of city and airport offices of airlines offering regular service to, from or within El Salvador.

American Airlines
Edificio La Centroamericana
Alameda Roosevelt 3107
City ☎: 298-0777
Airport ☎: 339-9253

COPA (Compañía Panameña de Aviación)
Alameda Roosevelt 2838 at 55ª Avenida Norte
City ☎: 223-2042 or 271-2333
Airport ☎: 339-9005

Continental Airlines
Edificio Torre Roble, Metrocentro
Boulevard Los Héroes
City ☎: 279-2233
Airport ☎: 339-9055

Iberia
Centro Comercial Plaza Jardín
Carretera a Santa Tecla
City ☎: 223-2711 or 223-2600

LACSA
43ª Avenida Norte 216
City ☎: 298-1322

TACA International Airlines
Edficio Caribe
Plaza Las Américas

City ☎: 298-5055, 298-5066 or 298-5077
Airport ☎: 339-9155

Transportes Aéreos de El Salvador (TAES)
Aeropuerto de Ilopango
☎ 295-0280, 295-0363, 295-0312 or 295-0349.

United Airlines
Edificio La Centroamericana
Alameda Roosevelt 3107
City ☎: 279-4469, 298-5503 or 279-3900
Airport ☎: 339-9234

■ **Long-Distance Telephone**

For international telephone calls, hotels often tack on a big supplement, and some hotels do not provide this service at all. The main alternatives are to call collect, to use a Call Direct service (see p 43), or to go to one of the offices of Antel, the national telephone company.

The main Antel office *(Calle Rubén Darío at 5ª Avenida Sur, open every day 6 a.m. to 10:30 p.m.)* is a big, intimidating, oppressive place wrapped in bureaucracy. The first step is to go to the main counter and request your call, stating how many minutes of calling time you want. Second, leave a deposit with the cashier. Third, wait for your name to be called by loudspeaker (the wait is usually five to ten minutes), along with the number of the phone cabin to which your call will be connected. Fourth, complete your call. Fifth, return to the cashier to collect what remains of your deposit.

We recommend instead going to the Antel branch office *(Mon to Sat 7 a.m. to 6:30 p.m., closed Sun)* in the Edificio Torre Roble, upstairs from the Metrocentro shopping centre,

Boulevard Los Héroes across from the Hotel Camino Real. Besides being air conditioned, it is smaller, less initimidating and less bureaucratic.

Fax messages can be sent from both offices.

Exploring

■ City Centre ★

The heart of San Salvador has largely been given over to street vendors, and many of its important buildings and plazas show serious signs of neglect, but it is worth visiting if only to imagine what it once looked like. Photos from early in the 20th century show a stylish city centre where the *bourgeoisie* felt quite at home, quite different from the current scene. The numbers after the attractions refer to the map of San Salvador.

The place to start is the **Catedral Metropolitana (1)** *(2ª Calle Oriente between Avenida Cuscatlán and 2ª Avenida Sur)*, a cavernous concrete structure with a high dome. The entrance faces **Plaza Barrios (2)**, the biggest public square but rather bare and desolate itself. Anyone expecting to see something ancient and ornate will be disappointed. This building is modern and as bare and unadorned as can be. In fact, construction was never completed because funds ran out after wealthy benefactors found themselves in growing disagreement with the local church hierarchy, who were coming to identify increasingly with the poor. The best time to visit is during Sunday mass, when the place fills with people and no longer looks so desolate. Almost all worshippers are poor people.

On the western side of Plaza Barrios is the **Palacio Nacional (3)**, which formerly housed the offices of top government officials. The building, with several ornate murals, was heavily damaged in the 1986 earthquake and lay abandoned for several years. More recently, restoration work was begun, but it has so far proceeded very slowly, and there is no clear idea what future purpose the building might serve. Two blocks east is **Plaza Libertad**, which has a monument to liberty and faces the nondescript **Iglesia El Rosario**.

Behind the cathedral, at the corner of Calle Delgado and 2ª Avenida Sur, is the **Teatro Nacional (4)** ★, which was very elegant in its day (it opened in 1917) and still is, with red velvet, ceiling murals and private boxes. There are occasional theatrical or musical performances here; listings are in the local newspapers. There used to be an elegant café on one side, but after surviving the civil war, earthquakes and goodness knows what else, it finally shut its doors in 1993. The theatre faces the smaller **Plaza Morazán**.

There are two important markets in the city centre. The **Mercado Ex-Cuartel (5)** ★, at Calle Delgado and 8ª Avenida Norte, is a good and inexpensive place to shop for handicrafts (see p 78). The **Mercado Central (6)**, three blocks south of Calle Rubén Darío between 7ª and 9ª Avenidas Sur, is where many people shop for food and basic household items.

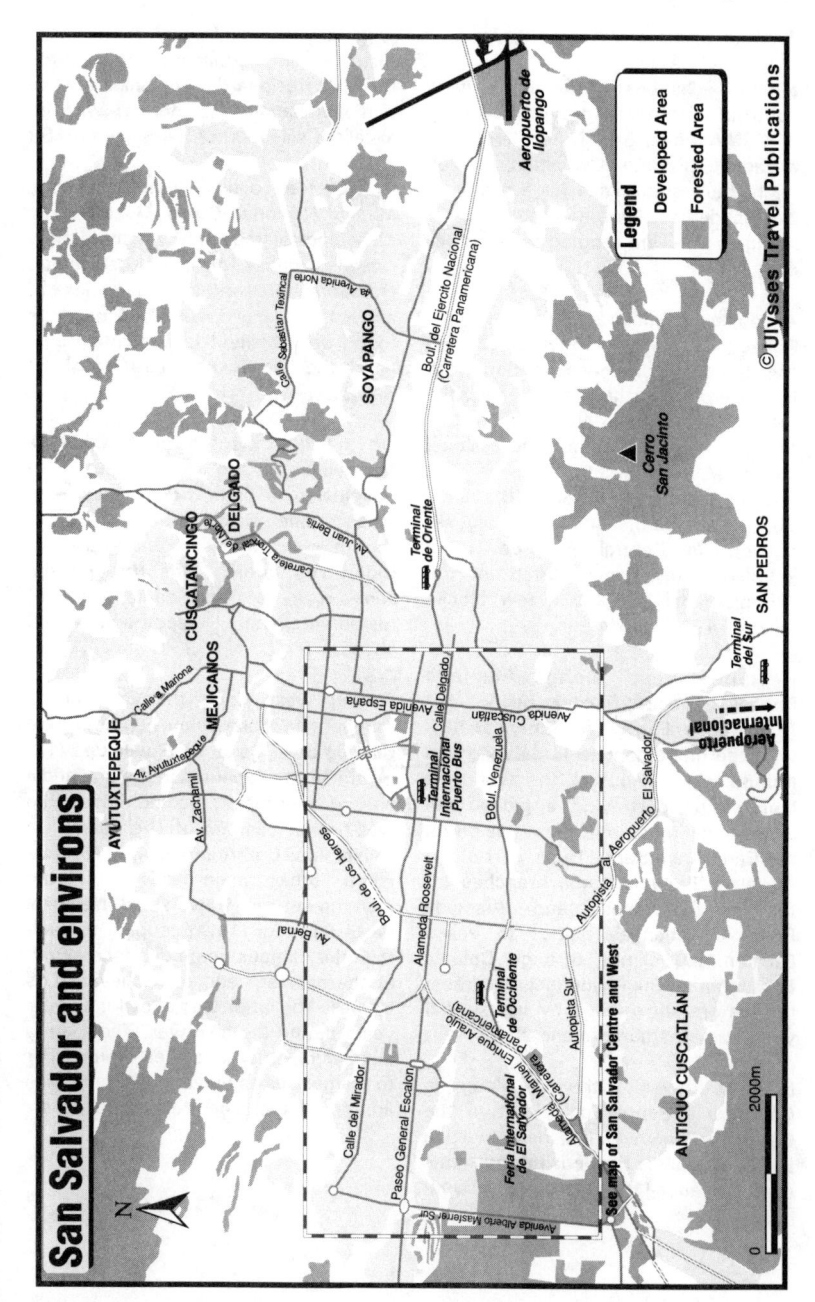

San Salvador and environs

Legend
- Developed Area
- Forested Area

© Ulysses Travel Publications

■ West of the City Centre ★

A few blocks west of the centre, lying south of Alameda Roosevelt and west of 25ª Avenida Sur, is the large and attractive **Parque Cuscatlán**, which might be a good place for a pleasant, tree-shaded stroll were it not for the muggers who are reputed to hang out here.

A couple of blocks south of Alameda Roosevelt, along 49ª Avenida Sur (which changes names from Boulevard Los Héroes further north), is the 30,000-seat **Estadio Nacional (7)**, one of two main venues for professional soccer (*fútbol*) in San Salvador. The newer **Estadio Cuscatlán (8)** holds 80,000 spectators and is the biggest stadium in Central America. It is situated a few blocks south of the Autopista del Sur and a few blocks west of 49ª Avenida Sur.

Heading west along Alameda Roosevelt, about 10 blocks beyond 49ª Avenida, is **Plaza Las Américas (9)**, with the monument to **El Salvador del Mundo** (the saviour of the world), a high statue portraying a globe with Jesus standing atop it. From this plaza, the Carretera a Santa Tecla, part of the Carretera Panamericana, branches off to the southwest and Alameda Roosevelt changes names to Paseo Escalón and climbs through **Colonia Escalón**, a swank residential area (most houses are surrounded by high walls) with many restaurants and shops.

In the southwest of the city, along the Carretera a Santa Tecla (part of the Carretera Panamericana) near Avenida La Revolución, is the **Feria Internacional de El Salvador (10)**, a large fairground with several exhibition halls, used for trade fairs. Adjacent to it is the **Mercado Nacional de Artesanías (11)** ★ (national handicrafts market) with an excellent selection of items (see p 78).

Across the road is what was the **Museo Nacional David Guzmán**, an archeological museum which is now closed because of structural faults. Outdoors in front are a series of ancient and enormous stone carvings found on an island in Lago de Güija, near the northwest corner of El Salvador.

On a hill at the top of Avenida La Revolución is the **Monumento a la Revolución**, a huge, brightly coloured mosaic panel. Below the monument is the intersection with Boulevard del Hipódromo, which runs through the *zona rosa*, a fashionable area of restaurants, bars, discotheques and shops.

Further west along the Carretera a Santa Tecla is the colourful and ornate **Basílica de la Ceiba de Guadalupe (12)** ★, the prettiest church in the city and a site of pilgrimage. Behind it lies the well-heeled campus of the Jesuit-run **Universidad Centroamericana (13)**. The city's other main university, the government-run **Universidad Nacional de El Salvador (14)**, occupies a much tawdrier campus some distance away, at the northern end of Boulevard Los Héroes. The latter was shut for several years during the civil war. There are a number of other institutes which refer to themselves as universities, but these are mostly technical training colleges.

Exploring 65

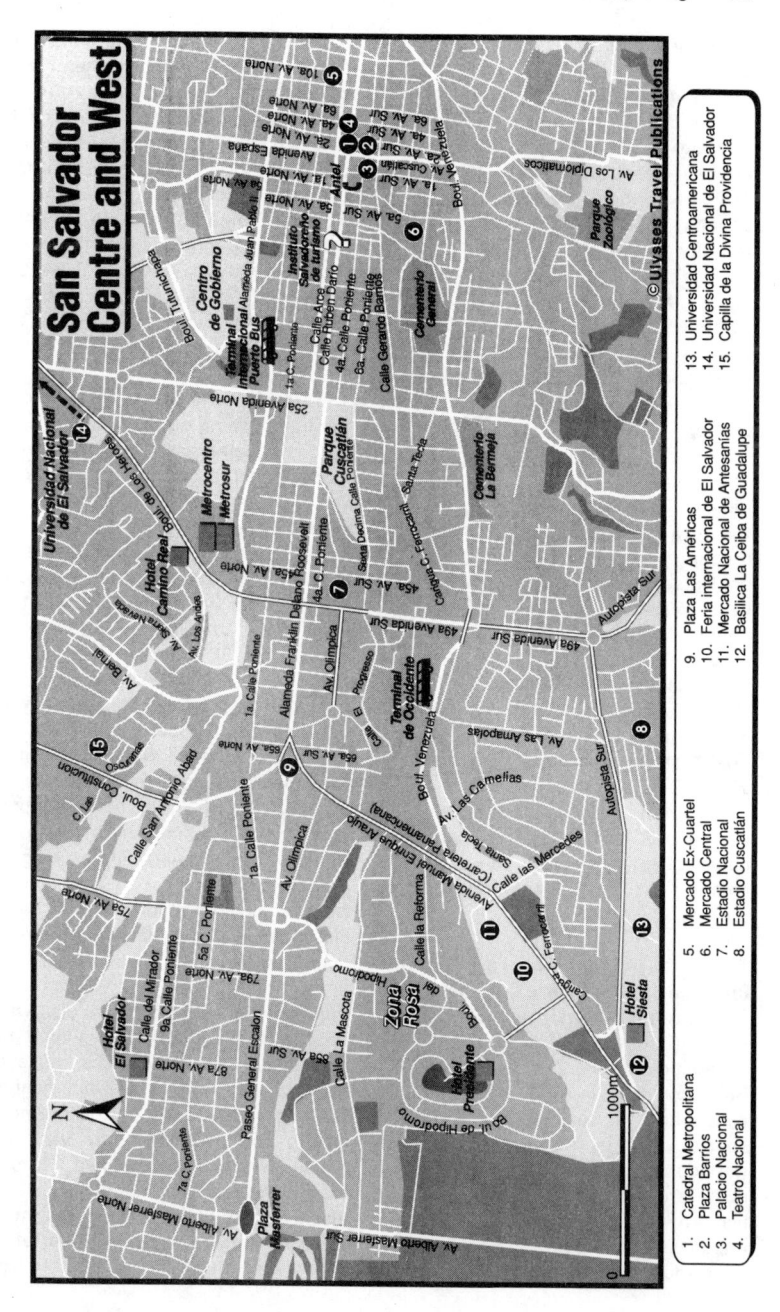

San Salvador Centre and West

1. Catedral Metropolitana
2. Plaza Barrios
3. Palacio Nacional
4. Teatro Nacional
5. Mercado Ex-Cuartel
6. Mercado Central
7. Estadio Nacional
8. Estadio Cuscatlán
9. Plaza Las Américas
10. Feria Internacional de El Salvador
11. Mercado Nacional de Antesanías
12. Basílica La Ceiba de Guadalupe
13. Universidad Centroamericana
14. Universidad Nacional de El Salvador
15. Capilla de la Divina Providencia

© Ulysses Travel Publications

Other Sights

The **Parque Zoológico Nacional** ★ *(Wed to Sun 8 a.m. to 4 p.m., ☎ 270-0823)* is a big tree-shaded area with several rare species from the cat family and brilliantly-plumed tropical birds. It is situated about 2 km (1¼ mi) south of the city centre, near the end of Calle Modelo, which can be reached by heading south along Avenida Cuscatlán or by taking bus route 2, marked Modelo. Just behind the zoo is the **Casa Presidencial**, the president's official residence, which is not open to the public.

The new **U.S. Embassy** is a sight to behold. The old one was pretty big, but the new one is enormous, especially in a country of only six million people. It consists of a great cluster of white and beige buildings inside a walled compound, easily visible from a distance. It does have architectural appeal, but its vast scale is a monument to Ronald Reagan's obsession with El Salvador. The embassy was built during Reagan's final years in office and inaugurated in 1989. It is situated in Colonia Santa Elena, on the southwestern edge of the city, and is serving as the anchor for new real estate developments that are creating yet further decentralization of the city.

The **Capilla de la Divina Providencia (15)** ★★ lies off the regular tourist route but will appeal to visitors with an interest in Salvadoran history or politics. Monseñor Oscar Arnulfo Romero, the late Roman Catholic archbishop of San Salvador, holds a special place in the recent history of the country. He came to be reviled by many among the wealthy because of his growing determination to nurture the cause of the poor, and he achieved martyrdom on March 24, 1980, when a trained assassin felled him with a single bullet through the heart as he celebrated mass. Contrary to the Hollywood version as told in the film *Romero*, he was gunned down not in San Salvador's cathedral but rather in this chapel on the grounds of the Hospital Divina Providencia, a hospital and orphanage run by Carmelite nuns. It is located on Avenida B at Calle Toluca, just off Boulevard Constitución in the northwestern part of the city, north of Colonia Escalón.

The Capilla de la Divina Providencia is the first building on the left after entering the hospital grounds. It is a bright, modern church, simple in its lines and very pure in its religious imagery, and at first glance it may seem rather ordinary. Even non-believers will find a visit to this chapel strangely moving thanks in part to an unadorned plaque at the base of the altar laid by the Carmelite sisters in 1987 on the seventh anniversary of the assassination, with the following quote from Romero: "Nadie tiene más amor que él que da la vida por sus amigos." ("Nobody has more love than he who gives his life for his friends.") At the rear of the church, near the entrance, is a photo of Romero taking part in a religious procession, and next to that a quote from remarks he made a month before his death in which he predicted what might happen.

Romero lived in a tiny house elsewhere on the hospital grounds, which has now been converted to a museum. Visitors may enter the main hospital building and ask one of the Carmelite sisters for permission to visit this house, which is kept locked. No contribution is solicited. In a glass case are displayed the blood-stained vestments worn by Romero at the moment of his death. Also on exhibit are posters from several countries in homage to him and some of his personal belongings, including a narrow bed, several religious objects, an old typewriter and many books. Asked if this was where he had lived, a Carmelite sister replied, "*Aquí él vive*" — he lives here. She stated this firmly in the present tense. To Romero's many admirers, his inspiration clearly lives on.

■ **Panchimalco** ★

This is an attractive village lying 14 km (9 mi) south of San Salvador, served by local bus 17 from the city centre. The inhabitants are mostly Indian, although traditional dress is not visible. The village has a very pretty white church facing its cobbled central plaza and several picturesque streets nearby. It lies below the Puerta del Diablo, the hilltop observation point at the southern edge of San Salvador. All around are beautiful vistas of hills and valleys. When travelling between San Salvador and La Libertad, there is a longer alternate route that passes through Panchimalco. The road between San Salvador passes near Parque Balboa and also passes by the **Gran Mirador de los Planes**, a lookout with magnificent views over the surrounding countryside.

■ **Lago de Ilopango** ★

Lago de Ilopango lies 16 km (10 mi) east of San Salvador and is readily visible from the Carretera Panamericana (local bus 15 from the centre of San Salvador). The lake is enormous, 12 km (7.5 mi) long and eight km (5 mi) wide, and it fills the crater of an extinct volcano. The highway runs along a high ridge overlooking the lake, and just below is the Vistalago restaurant and hotel (see p 72); from the dining room there are superb views over the lake

and the surrounding hills. There is a *turicentro* (see below) down at the base of the road near the village of **Apulo** for those who care to swim, but the lake is really best appreciated from above.

Parks and Beaches

Parque Balboa ★ *(admission $0.60 per person plus $0.60 per vehicle)* is an enormous park, 28 hectares (69 acres) in area, perched at the far southern edge of San Salvador, reached by heading south along Avenida Cuscatlán from the city centre or by bus route 12, marked Mil Cumbres. The park has many gardens, pathways and bicycle trails, as well as several statues and a children's playground. At the far end of the park is the **Puerta del Diablo** ★★, a series of high ridges which provide spectacular views over a great distance. The name means the devil's door.

Los Chorros ★★ *($0.60 per person plus $0.60 per vehicle; open every day 8 a.m. to 6 p.m.)* is a *turicentro* 18 km (11 mi) northwest of San Salvador along the Carretera Panamericana and can be reached by bus 201 to Santa Ana from the Terminal de Oriente in San Salvador (look for buses marked *Ordinario*; those marked *Directo* may not stop), or by local bus 79, which runs from the city centre along Alameda Roosevelt. Los Chorros is a series of magnificent natural pools and cascades surrounded by high ridges and tropical vegetation. There are also artificial pools, gardens and snack bars.

Along the north shore of **Lago de Ilopango** is the Apulo *turicentro ($0.60 per person plus $0.60 per vehicle; open* every day 8 a.m. to 6 p.m.), down a long, steep road from the Carretera Panamericana 16 km (10 mi) east of San Salvador and can be reached by local bus 15 from the city centre. Besides lake access, the *turicentro* offers gardens, snack bars and lockers.

Outdoor Activities

Hiking

It is possible to climb the **San Salvador volcano**, also known as El Boquerón, from **Santa Tecla** (officially called Nueva San Salvador) which has practically become a suburb and lies to the west along the Carretera Panamericana. Bus 101 runs frequently to Santa Tecla from the centre of San Salvador and along Alameda Roosevelt, and from there bus 103 runs hourly partway up the slope of the volcano. From there it is a half-hour climb to the top and about two hours around the rim of the volcano. There is also a path descending into the volcano along its forested inner slopes.

Accommodation

Hotels in San Salvador cover a broad range, from the five-star to the truly dismal. The hotel scene is a faithful reflection of the way the city has evolved over the last several decades, with money migrating toward the outskirts and the city centre being abandoned to the poor. There is no single district of the city which can be pointed to as a hotel zone, and lodgings are widely scattered, although there are several areas with clusters of small, low-priced hotels.

One area to look for lower-priced lodgings is within a short radius of the corner of 1ª Calle Poniente and 17ª Avenida Norte, just west of the city centre. Another area, this one down a peg or two and not at all safe at night, is around the Mercado Ex-Cuartel, near the corner of 8ª Avenida Norte and Calle Delgado. Yet another is along Calle Concepción, east of the centre; hotels there tend to be crude and unpleasant, and again the area is unsafe at night. For accommodations in the lower-to-middle range, there are several possibilities in middle-class neighbourhoods surrounding the upper-range Hotel Camino Real, in the area near Boulevard Los Héroes. The Camino Real is a landmark in its own right.

The city's top-of-the-line hostelries are scattered far apart. A big increase in the number of business visitors in recent years has created occasional shortages of hotel space in this category, producing a ripple effect that has sent some visitors to hotels a notch or two below what they might have preferred. Still, there normally should be little trouble finding suitable accommodations in most categories on any given date. Prices are generally lower than what visitors might expect to encounter in North America or Europe but higher than they have been in the recent past.

The more expensive hotels tend to quote their prices without including the tax (10% at the time of writing), while tax is nearly always included in the prices of other categories of hotels. For the sake of consistency, we show all prices here with tax included.

Hotels In or Near the City Centre

Hotel Imperial *($6 per person with private bath, $4 per person with shared bath; Calle Concepción 659, ☎ 222-4920)* is a very friendly but somewhat noisy spot with dark, basic rooms and cars parked in the courtyard.

There are several other small hotels nearby, among them are the seedy and unpleasant **Hotel Yucatán** *($3 per person, Calle Concepción 673)*, and most are even worse. The area is not at all safe at night.

Hotel San Carlos *($6 per person; Calle Concepción 121 at 2ª Avenida Norte)* is a tiny, dark, unpleasant place in a seedy area. We mention it only because Tica-Bus uses this hotel as its San Salvador terminal and many arriving passengers end up staying here. Unless money is very tight, it is better to flag a taxi and head elsewhere.

Hotel Panamericano *($10 ⊗, $14 to $17 ≡; TV; 8ª Avenida Sur 113 near Calle Delgado, ☎ 222-2959)* is a friendly spot, but its 26 rooms, which vary in size, are crudely furnished. It is located near the Mercado Ex-Cuartel, in an area that is lively by day but dangerous at night.

Hotel Nuevo Panamericano, next door, is similar. Other modest hotels in this area include **Hotel León** and **Hotel Custodio**, both near 10ª Avenida Sur and Calle Delgado.

Hotel Centro *($14, VI - MC; TV, ☎, ⊗; 9ª Avenida Sur 410 between 4ª Calle Poniente and Calle General Barrios; ☎ 271-5045)* is a simple, friendly spot near the central market, but the neighbourhood is rough at night. The 28 rooms are small and have no hot water.

There is a small courtyard with hanging plants.

Family Guest Home *($14 single, $20 double; 1ª Calle Poniente bis 925 between 15ª and 17ª Avenidas Norte, ☎ 221-2349 or 222-1902)* is located a few blocks west of the city centre in a rundown area. It has 10 simple rooms with fans, a lounge with television, a small dining room, and an old-fashioned atmosphere.

Hotel American Guest House *($16 single, $20 double, VI - MC - AE - DC; 17ª Avenida Norte 119 between 1ª Calle Poniente and Calle Arce, ☎ 271-0224)* is situated a short distance west of the city centre in a rundown area. The hotel has an old-fashioned atmosphere and matching decor. There are 11 rooms and a snack counter.

Hotel Fénix *($23, VI - MC - AE, 10%-surcharge for use of credit cards; 17ª Avenida Norte at 1ª Calle Poniente, ☎ 271-1279)* has eight big, old-fashioned rooms with fans and simple but comfortable furnishings. The hotel is situated just west of the city centre, in a rather rundown area, but the staff and atmosphere are friendly.

Hotel Ritz Continental *($31 single, $36 double, VI - MC - AE - DC; ≡, TV, ☎, ≈, ℜ; 7ª Avenida Sur 219 near Calle Rubén Darío, ☎ 222-0033, ⇄ 222-9842)* is situated right in the turbulent city centre. Like its surroundings, it has seen better days, but the owners are attempting valiantly to maintain it, and service is friendly. Rooms and corridors are spacious, but furnishings are rather chintzy. The pool area is grubby.

Hotel Internacional Puerto Bus *($45, VI - MC; ≡, TV; Alameda Juan Pablo II at*

19ª Avenida Norte, above the international bus terminal, ☎ 221-1000, ⇄ 222-2138) is a friendly spot with 38 simply but attractively furnished rooms. They vary in size, and some have good views of the San Salvador volcano. The location is convenient for those arriving or leaving on an international bus, and though it is near the Centro de Gobierno, it feels a bit remote. There are restaurants directly below.

■ **Hotels Near Boulevard Los Héroes**

Hotel Florida Guest House ($12 single, $18 double; Pasaje Los Almendros 115, Urbanización La Florida, reached via Pasaje Las Palmeras behind Boulevard Los Héroes, ☎ 226-1858) is a friendly, family-run hotel with 12 pleasant rooms set in a big modern house on a quiet but hard-to-find side street in a safe neighbourhood a few blocks from the Hotel Camino Real.

Hotel Occidental ($17; 49ª Avenida Norte near Alameda Roosevelt, ☎ 223-7715) looks quite foreboding from the outside but has a pleasant, homey feel inside, with big, cheerful rooms. It is situated a few blocks south of the Hotel Camino Real.

Hotel Happy House Guest Home ($19 single, $22 double; VI - MC - AE - DC; Avenida Los Sisimiles 2951, Colonia Miramonte, ☎ 226-6866) has a small restaurant and big rooms with rather tacky furnishings. The district lies near the Hotel Camino Real.

Hotel and Restaurant Good Luck ($32, VI - MC; ⊗, TV; Avenida Los Sisimiles 2943, Colonia Miramonte, ☎ 226-8287) has 16 simple but comfortably furnished rooms, although thin curtains fail to keep out much light. The restaurant has a Chinese menu. The district lies near the Hotel Camino Real.

Hotel Casa Grande Miramonte ($30 single $40 double ⊗, $40 single, $60 double ≡, VI - MC - AE; Calle Los Sisimiles y Final Pasaje Los Cedros 138B, Colonia Miramonte, ☎ 274-7450 or 274-7478, ⇄ 274-7471) has 20 rooms of varying size facing an inner garden with a fountain. Rooms have television and rather plain white and orange decor. The district lies near the Hotel Camino Real.

Hotel Alameda ($72, VI - MC - AE - DC; ≡, TV, ☎, ≈, bar, ℜ; Alameda Roosevelt 2305 at 43ª Avenida Sur, ☎ 279-0299, ⇄ 279-3011) is a friendly spot with comfortable but nondescript rooms and a central location about midway between the city centre and the more opulent districts. Rooms facing the street are noisy. The hotel has a pool bar and possibly the best hotel restaurant in the city.

Hotel Camino Real ($143 for regular rooms, $165 for executive club rooms, VI - MC - AE - DC; ≡, cable TV, ☎, business centre, ≈, ℜ, including 24-hour coffee shop, two bars; Boulevard Los Héroes, ☎ 279-3888 or 298-1333, ⇄ 223-5660, reservations in U.S. or Canada (800) 228-3000) is about as centrally located as any hotel in the city, facing two big shopping centres and situated midway between the main government buildings and the more fashionable residential areas. This is a modern, eight-story building, with a carefully landscaped area in back containing a large pool and an outdoor dining area. The regular rooms are fairly ordinary in decor, while the executive club rooms are decidedly more elegant and provide the use of a lounge with light breakfasts and snacks. There are 235 rooms in all. The hotel is not always as quiet as some guests may prefer: although it is well set back from the street, noise from passing traffic can still penetrate rooms facing that way. Rooms on the other side facing the pool and mountains provide a more appealing view but can be noisy on Wednesday evenings when the hotel hosts an outdoor Mexican barbecue with mariachis performing. During the civil war, this hotel was the semi-official headquarters of the foreign press corps, with the coffee shop buzzing with correspondents at all hours and rooms on the third floor converted to offices for television networks and news services. These have long since reverted to ordinary hotel rooms.

■ Hotels in Colonia Escalón

Novo Apart-Hotel *($54-$73, VI - MC - AE - DC; ≡, TV, ☏, ₡, ≈; Final 61ª Avenida Norte, Colonia Escalón, ☏ 279-0099, ⇄ 279-2688)* has 50 suites in three different sizes. Decor varies, but all have kitchenettes. Weekly and monthly rates are available, and the hotel caters in part to long-staying guests. It has a large garden and pool, and the outdoor corridor leading to some rooms faces a high, fern-covered wall. A small restaurant offers light breakfasts and lunches only. The hotel is situated on a secluded side street in the Escalón residential area. It takes a few minutes to get a taxi.

Ramada Inn *($73, VI - MC - AE - DC; ≡, TV, ☏, balconies, ≈; 85ª Avenida Sur near Paseo Escalón, ☏ 279-1820 or 279-3911, ⇄ 279-1889)* has 23 quiet and fairly ordinary rooms. It is well situated in an area with many restaurants.

Hotel Terraza *($88, VI - MC - AE - DC; ≡, TV, ☏, ≈, ℛ, bar; 85ª Avenida Sur near Paseo Escalón, ☏ 279-0044, ⇄ 223-2323)* was under renovation during 1994. The renovated rooms are pleasantly decorated in green tones. A corner table in each room can be used as a desk. The pool is in a grassy area with a thatch-shaded bar. The hotel has 80 rooms and is well situated, with many restaurants nearby.

Hotel El Salvador *($80 VIP tower, $130 main tower, VI - MC - AE - DC; ≡, TV, ☏, ≈, ℛ, bar; 89ª Avenida Norte at 11ª Calle Poniente, Colonia Escalón, ☏ 279-0777; ⇄ 223-2901)* has rooms in two towers situated on different sides of the pool. Rooms in the main tower are newly renovated; furnishings are elegant and include wooden dressers. The VIP tower is less elegant but quite acceptable, and good for the price. Even-numbered rooms in both towers provide views of the San Salvador volcano. This hotel, formerly the Sheraton, is situated at a high elevation deep within Colonia Escalón, one of the wealthiest residential areas.

■ Hotels in the Southwest of the City

Hotel Siesta *($90, VI - MC - AE - DC; ≡, TV, ☏, ≈, ℛ, bar; Autopista Sur next to Basílica de la Ceiba de Guadalupe, ☏ 279-0377 or 279-0384, ⇄ 224-6575)* has 69 rooms and is expanding to 120. Rooms are pleasantly furnished, and the restaurant faces the landscaped pool area. The location, near the edge of a highway in the southwest of the city, can be slightly awkward.

Hotel Presidente *($143, VI - MC - DC; ≡, ☏, TV, ≈, bar, ℛ; Colonia San Benito, ☏ 279-4444, ⇄ 223-4912)* is perched on a quiet hilltop near San Salvador's monument to the revolution, not far from the Zona Rosa with its many restaurants. This four-story semicircular building has 244 rooms with good views of the city and mountains, along with a big pool and outdoor dining area. Buffets are offered at breakfast and lunch, while supper is à la carte only. Long, gloomy corridors lead to the rooms, which are carpeted and furnished in modern style, with some walls of painted concrete block. Service is friendly.

■ **Hotel at Lago de Ilopango**

Hotel Vistalago *($14 single, $17 double, VI - MC - AE - DC; ≡, ≈, ℜ; Carretera Apulo kilómetro 12.5, Ilopango,* ☎ *295-0532)* has superb views of Lago de Ilopango. It is situated just off the Carretera Panamericana high above the lake, in an area just beyond the eastern outskirts of San Salvador. It is certainly very good value for money, although its 32 rooms seem to be furnished in rather haphazard fashion. The out-of-the-way location makes for a slow commute to the city.

■ **Restaurants**

The restaurant scene in San Salvador has something to offer almost everyone. There are several "restaurant rows" with big concentrations of eating places. Some of the top restaurants are located along **Paseo Escalón**, in the district of the same name. An adjacent area called Colonia La Mascota also has several interesting restaurants. Boulevard del Hipódromo and nearby streets, in the so-called *zona rosa* in the southwest of the city has an impressive array of restaurants ranging from casual taco-and-beer joints to some of the finest restaurants in town. In the *zona rosa*, restaurants are close enough together that it is possible to stroll and look around before deciding where to eat. Most are open late.

Reservations are rarely required, although at the more elegant restaurants it may sometimes be a good idea to book ahead, especially on weekends. Dress is casual at most spots, but shorts and T-shirts are definitely frowned upon at the fancier establishments.

For something light and quick, the **Metrosur** shopping centre near the Hotel Camino Real has a food court with 18 outlets whose offerings range from tacos to fish and chips. There is an attractive, open-air seating area. At the far corner of the shopping centre is a giant branch of the Pollo Campero fried chicken empire.

Fried chicken, pizza and hamburger joints, many with familiar American names, are found in several parts of the city.

■ **Restaurants In or Near the City Centre**

There are many humble restaurants scattered around the city centre offering lunches with *comida a la vista*, meaning that dishes are already prepared and customers point to what they want. These tend to be very inexpensive but not very comfortable.

Los Entremeses de Federico *(most items $2; Mon to Sat 11:30 a.m. to 2 p.m.; 1ª Calle Poniente between 13ª and 15ª Avenidas Norte,* ☎ *221-2016)* is one of the few places worth mentioning near the city centre. Set in a pleasant, tree-shaded courtyard, it offers buffet lunches with salads and dishes such as stuffed peppers or chicken lasagna. Like everything around, it is a bit rundown.

La Zanahoria *(most items $2-$5; Mon to Fri 8 a.m. to 6 p.m., until 2 p.m. Sat, closed Sun; Calle Arce 1144 between 19ª and 21ª Avenidas Norte)* is a big open-air restaurant with a broad choice of vegetarian dishes (*zanahoria* means carrot). It is situated a few blocks west of the city centre.

■ **Restaurants Near the Hotel Camino Real**

The street directly behind the Hotel Camino Real, near Boulevard Los Héroes, has a row of casual, inexpensive restaurants that include **Asia** for Chinese food, **Taco Taco** for tacos and *pupusas*, **La Parrillada** for meats and seafood, and several others.

Among these others is **Los Mariscos** *(main courses $3-$5, VI - MC; 11:30 a.m. to 11:30 p.m.; ☎ 226-9278)*, which has an open terrace with wood tables and benches and remarkably inexpensive prices for fish and seafood.

Another is **Hola Beto's** *(main courses $4-$7, VI - MC - AE - DC; open 11 a.m. to 10:30 p.m.; ☎ 226-8621)*, a big, informal spot with wooden benches, awful music and a very broad selection of seafood cocktails and *ceviches* (marinated fish or seafood), along with seafood soups and main dishes including mussels and clams, as well as spaghetti and pizza.

Ay Jalisco *(items average about $3; open every day 12 p.m. to 11 p.m.; Pasaje Las Palmeras, off Boulevard Los Héroes, ☎ 226-2689)* is a big, casual open-air restaurant serving tacos and other Mexican *antojitos*, which are light dishes containing meat or cheese.

El Café de Don Pedro *(most items $2-$7; open 24 hours Alameda Roosevelt at 39ª Avenida)* is an inexpensive open-air restaurant set back just far enough from a busy roadway to avoid the bus fumes. It offers meat, sandwiches, Mexican dishes and a superb *crema de frijoles*, a thick, rich soup of black beans and avocado.

La Mansión *(main courses $5-$11; open every day 6:30 a.m. to 10:30 p.m. 43ª Avenida Sur at Alameda Roosevelt, in the Hotel Alameda, ☎ 279-0299)* is quite possibly the best hotel restaurant in San Salvador, in part because it does not feel like a hotel restaurant. It is set in an old mansion that was incorporated into the Hotel Alameda and has a series of small dining rooms with some interesting nooks and crannies. The menu concentrates on grilled meats and shrimps and includes a cream of seafood soup with shrimp and lobster for $4 and a generous portion of pork loin in egg batter for $6. Breakfasts here are also good.

Pueblo Viejo *(main courses $5-$10, VI - MC - AE - DC; every day 7 a.m. to midnight in the Metrosur shopping centre on Boulevard Los Héroes, ☎ 298-5318)* is elaborately decorated with village scenes and colonial-style painted stucco. It has a dark interior dining room and an outdoor terrace subjected to traffic noise and fumes. The menu concentrates on seafood cocktails ($3-$6) and a wide variety of steaks ($7-$10).

■ **Restaurants in the *Zona Rosa***

The *zona rosa* is situated in Colonia San Benito in the southwestern part of the city. The nearest landmark is the Hotel Presidente.

Espresso Americano *(main courses $5-$8, VI - MC - AE - DC; Calle La Refor-*

ma just off Boulevard del Hipódromo, zona rosa) bills itself as an Italo-American eatery. It is a trendy open-air spot with soft jazz. The menu includes sandwiches and quiche, as well as chicken, shrimp and beef dishes.

Osteria dei Cuattro Gatti (main courses $5-$8, VI - MC - AE - DC; Calle La Reforma near Boulevard del Hipódromo, zona rosa, ☎ 223-6027 or 223-1625) is possibly the most sophisticated Italian restaurant in El Salvador. It is set in a series of small, elegant dining rooms along with a cosy bar. Appetizers ($3 to $5) include carpaccio, seafood salad, fried squid and porcini mushroom pancakes along with salads and soups. Among the pasta dishes ($5 to $7) are gnocchi, tortellini and spaghetti with lobster. Main courses concentrate on fish, shrimp and steak. There is a special daytime menu that changes weekly. The restaurant opens for lunch Monday to Friday and for supper Monday to Saturday.

Matsuri Sushi-Bar (main courses $6-$12, VI - MC - AE - DC; Bouelvard del Hipódromo 230, zona rosa) has an upstairs open-air terrace and wooden benches, with a menu devoted to fish and seafood. Items include seafood cocktails and ceviches (marinated fish or seafood) for $4 to $7, elaborate seafood soups ($5 to $9), and barbecued fish plus a wide variety of seafood ($6 to $12).

Méditerranée (main courses $5 to $14, VI - MC - AE - DC; every day 7 a.m. to 1 a.m., later on weekends; Boulevard del Hipódromo 131, zona rosa, ☎ 223-6137) is a casual, open-air seafood restaurant facing the street. The menu includes seafood cocktails, ceviches (marinated fish or seafood), seafood soup, several preparations of squid, shrimp or lobster as well as fresh fish.

Basilea (main courses $7-$11, VI - MC - AE - DC; Boulevard del Hipódromo 520, zona rosa, ☎ 223-6818) is an enchanting spot with a garden café and an elegant indoor dining room. Besides steak and shrimp dishes, it offers a variety of appetizers and a small selection of vegetarian dishes. It also offers an elaborate choice of cakes, ice creams and coffees.

■ Restaurants in Colonia Escalón and Colonia La Mascota

Sambuca (most items $4-$7; Mon to Sat 11 a.m. to 3 p.m. and 6 p.m. to 11 p.m., closed Sunday; 85ª Avenida at Calle del Mirador, Colonia Escalón, ☎ 223-2458) calls itself an Italian bistro, with a menu concentrating on pizzas and pastas. It is a casual spot with wood benches and an outdoor terrace.

Asia (main courses $4-$7, VI - MC; open every day 12 p.m. to 3 p.m. and 6 p.m. to 10 p.m. Paseo Escalón 4352, ☎ 223-5700) has a fairly ordinary dining room and varied but standard menu, with a good selection of seafood items.

China Town (main courses $5-$8, VI - MC - AE - DC; open every day 12 p.m. to 11:30 p.m.; Paseo Escalón 4710 near 91ª Avenida Norte, ☎ 224-2889) has a simple dining room with white tablecloths and a conventional, U.S.-style Chinese menu.

La Pampa Argentina (main courses $5-$10, VI - MC - AE - DC; open every day 12 p.m. to 2:30 p.m. and 6 p.m. to 10:30 p.m., until 11 p.m. Fri and Sat, until 9:30 p.m. Sun; near the top of Paseo Escalón, two blocks before Plaza Masferrer, ☎ 279-1185) is among the best values on the local restaurant scene. It has a friendly, rustic atmosphere, with an all-wood interior. Grilled meats, Argentine-style, are the specialty. Examples are an eight-ounce (225-gram) pork filet for $5 and a mixed grill for $9. Grilled shrimp are $11.

Dallas *(main courses $5-$12, VI - MC - AE - DC; open every day 12 p.m. to 11:30 p.m., until 1 a.m. Fri and Sat; 79ª Avenida Sur 48, Colonia La Mascota,* ☎ *279-4043 or 279-3551)* is a Tex-Mex steakhouse with a wooden interior and a rustic atmosphere. The menu includes seafood cocktails, steaks, ribs, chicken, shrimps and fish. There are special family deals on Sundays.

La Diligencia *(main courses $8-$13, VI - MC - AE - DC; open every day 7 a.m. to 11:30 p.m.; Paseo Escalón near 83ª Avenida Sur,* ☎ *224-2716)* is an American-style steakhouse with a dark, comfortable interior. The menu includes lobster in cream sauce and grilled shrimp as well as an array of steaks and mixed grills.

El Árbol de Dios *(appetizers $4-$6, main courses $7-$12, VI - MC - AE - DC; Mon to Sat 12 p.m. to 10 p.m., until 11 p.m. Fri and Sat; Final Calle La Mascota at Avenida Masferer Sur, Urbanización el Maquilishuat,* ☎ *224-6200)* is attached to the art gallery of the same name, devoted to the work of Salvadoran painter Fernando Llort. The restaurant has a cosy dining room and two outdoor terraces, with decorative curtains and blue tablecloths. Examples of appetizers are mushrooms stuffed with crab and cream of seafood soup. For main courses, the menu concentrates on the usual steak, fish, shrimp and chicken dishes.

Fonda del Sol *(appetizers $4-$9, main courses $8-$13, VI - MC - AE - DC; open every day 12 p.m. to 3 p.m., 7 p.m. to midnight; Paseo Escalón 4920 near 91ª Avenida Norte,* ☎ *223-0928)* is one of the most elegant restaurants in El Salvador. Its formal dining room has peach-coloured walls and tablecloths. Appetizers include smoked salmon, *carpaccio*, crabcakes, and crepes with *huitlacoche* fungus. A house specialty, *corvina Fonda del Sol*, is fish grilled with olive oil, cheese, almonds and asparagus. The menu also includes pastas, *risotto*, shrimp and steak.

El Cortijo Español *(main courses $8-$13, VI - MC - AE - DC; open every day 6:30 p.m. to midnight or later; 79ª Avenida Sur near Pasaje a la Colonia Mascota,* ☎ *223-8382)* consists of a series of small dining rooms in brick, stucco and wood with dark tablecloths and the inevitable bullfight posters. The menu concentrates on Spanish dishes. Appetizers include smoked ham with melon, garlic mushrooms, *gazpacho* and cream of seafood soup. Main courses include steak and chicken but run heavily to fish and seafood, including a seafood mixed grill and *paella*.

El Bodegón *(main courses $8-$16, VI - MC - DC; Mon to Sat 12 p.m. to 3 p.m. and 6 p.m. to 11:30 p.m.; Paseo Escalón near 77ª Avenida Norte,* ☎ *223-1691)* is a graceful spot with a series of four dining rooms, elegant furniture, wine racks lining one wall and, incongruously, cheap industrial carpeting. The menu is thoroughly Spanish. Appetizers include mushrooms in cream sauce and tripes *a la Madrileña*. Among main courses are garlic shrimp, *paella*, kidneys *al Jerez* and seafood casserole. The owner, however, seems rather irascible.

■ Restaurants Elsewhere

Los Capulines *(most items $2-$4; open every day 3 p.m. to 2 a.m., later on busy nights; San Antonio Abad at Boulevard Constitución, across from an Esso gas station)* is a big, open-air bar and restaurant with hanging lanterns and a cheerful, rustic atmosphere. It offers a variety of *bocas*, hearty snacks of the type the Spanish call *tapas*, including preparations of fish, shrimp and *tesquite*, a dish of cornmeal and pork. It tends to draw an after-hours crowd and gets lively late in the evening. San Antonio Abad is a western extension of Alameda Juan Pablo II and runs north of Colonia Escalón.

Vistalago *(main courses $4-$9, VI - MC - AE - DC; Carretera Apulo kilómetro 2.5, ☎ 295-0532)* is a scenic spot for a breakfast or lunch with a breath-taking view over Lago de Ilopango. (At supper it is too dark to see anything.) The restaurant and adjoining hotel are situated just off the Carretera Panamericana high above the lake, a short distance beyond the eastern outskirts of San Salvador. Seafood cocktails are about $3, and main courses include meat, shrimp, sandwiches, spaghetti and a somewhat muddy-tasting lake fish called *guapote*.

Entertainment

The entertainment scene in San Salvador is stymied by several factors. One is the legendary clannishness of wealthy Salvadorans, whose entertainment often consists of visits with family and friends. A second is the poverty that afflicts a majority of the population, leaving them with little money to spend on anything beyond basic necessities. A third is the fear of crime. Despite this, there are signs of life after dusk, as well as entertainment possibilities during daylight hours.

■ Spectator Sports

El Salvador's favourite form of entertainment is soccer, known as *fútbol* and practically the national religion. Professional matches are presented at the **Estadio Cuscatlán**, which holds 80,000 spectators and is the biggest stadium in Central America. It is situated a few blocks south of the Autopista del Sur and a few blocks west of 49ª Avenida Sur. Other matches are held at the 30,000-seat **Estadio Nacional**, situated on 49ª Avenida Sur, a couple of blocks south of Alameda Roosevelt. Tickets are inexpensive. For information on schedules, consult local newspapers, or ask taxi drivers or male hotel clerks, who will tell you when their favourite teams are playing.

■ Cinema and Theatre

Another place for afternoon or evening entertainment is the **cinema** (called *cine* in Spanish, pronounced SEE-nay). There are several big movie theatres in San Salvador. Listings appear each day in the newspapers. Most American and other foreign-language films are presented in their original language and subtitled rather than dubbed in Spanish, making them more accessible to visitors. One of the more comfortable, and more comfortably situated, cinemas is the four-screen Cine Caribe, facing Plaza Las Américas, where Alameda Roosevelt changes names to Paseo Escalón and meets the Carretera a Santa Tecla. It is easy to find taxis after the showings.

The **Teatro Nacional** in the old city centre behind the cathedral, at the corner of Calle Delgado and 2ª Avenida Sur, presents occasional plays or concerts, usually starting in late afternoon so that patrons can clear out by early evening, before the nearby streets get dangerous. Again, consult newspaper listings, or inquire at the tourism office. The Café del Teatro, which used to present folk singing and poetry recitals, has been shut.

■ **Bars, Cafés and Discotheques**

La Luna *(Calle Berlín, two blocks from Boulevard Los Héroes, between the Hotel Camino Real and the Universidad Nacional)* is a lively café frequented by artists and intellectuals, some of them sympathetic to the left-wing FMLN. It has also become a minor tourist haunt.

The *zona rosa* (literally, pink zone), the area centred on Boulevard del Hipódromo in Colonia San Benito in the southwestern part of the city, has many restaurants and bars, as well as several discotheques (among them **Le Club**, **Calipso** and **Mario's**), and is lively at night. The discotheques are especially popular with young people from wealthy families, known sneeringly as *los chicos plásticos*, a term that needs no translation. But they are far from the only ones who go there, and it is among the few areas where it is safe to wander after dark. There are restaurants and bars to fit almost every wallet, and some of them are mentioned in the restaurant section above.

For something more sophisticated and more authentically Latin American, the area to head to is a two-block stretch of Boulevard Los Héroes across from the Hospital Benjamin Bloom, about midway between the Hotel Camino Real and the campus of the Universidad Nacional de El Salvador, where a cluster of big open-air bars and restaurants present live salsa and other musical forms on stage, with busy dance floors below. These tend to draw a young adult crowd. Bands vary in talent, but some of them are very good, and things get lively late in the evening, especially on weekends. Mondays and Tuesdays tend to be quiet. The music can be heard from the street, and this is one way to gauge whether it is worth entering a particular spot. Most of them are listed here. Taxis are readily available on the street outside, which is no small consideration in San Salvador at night.

Villa Fiesta *(Mon to Sat 6 p.m. to 1 a.m., until 3 a.m. Fri and Sat; live bands from 8:30 p.m. until shortly before closing)* claims to draw some of the best performers of salsa, merengue, *cumbia* and romantic ballads. By management decree, there is no hard rock! Cover and minimum vary according to the night of the week and the band that is performing. Beer costs $1.60 and cocktails are double that. Meals cost $6-$8.

Las Antorchas *(every day 10 a.m. to dawn, live music from 8 p.m. to 3 a.m.)* also offers salsa, merengue and *cumbia* bands. There is a $4 minimum, which is nearly enough for three beers here, plus a $2 cover from Thursday to Saturday. Meals and sandwiches are available.

El Corral *(every day 11:30 a.m. to 2 a.m., live music from 8 p.m. to closing)* is yet another salsa, merengue and *cumbia* place. There is a $4 minimum plus a $3 cover Friday and Saturday. Food is available, and beer is as little as $1, depending on the hour.

El Malibú *(Mon to Sat 12 p.m. to 1 a.m., live music from 8 p.m. to 1 a.m.)* strays from the norm and presents rock bands. Seating is on two levels. There is a $1 cover and no minimum. Beer is $1.20, and a limited menu is offered.

$ Shopping

■ Handicrafts

San Salvador is where visitors can find souvenirs and handicrafts from all over the country and shop for them in venues ranging from open-air bazaars to air-conditioned boutiques. It may be helpful to save most shopping until a day or two before departure to avoid having to store purchases or lug them around.

A very obvious place to look for handicrafts is the **Mercado Nacional de Artesanías** (National Handicrafts Market), situated in the southwest of the city along the Carretera a Santa Tecla next to the Feria Internacional de El Salvador. Here stalls are set in neat rows with a wide array of merchandise, including brightly hand-painted wooden objects from La Palma, ceramics from Ilobasco, basketware from Nahuizalco, and much, much more. Visitors will find a broad selection of the famous Salvadoran beach towels which are decorative enough to be used as wall hangings. Some of them are based on the colourful and whimsical portraits of rural life produced at La Palma, and a few are available also in the form of bathrobes. Other stalls sell hand-woven textiles, embroidered clothing, leather goods of many descriptions, jewellery, and stuffed toys, some resembling colourful tropical birds. Shoppers must be prepared to bargain. Credit cards are accepted at a few stalls.

Bargain-hunters may want to head to the **Mercado Ex-Cuartel** (*cuartel* means army barracks, and the site was once occupied by barracks), situated in the city centre at the corner of 8ª Avenida Norte and Calle Delgado. This is a vast indoor bazaar, and it is often possible to get lower prices on many of the same items sold at the Mercado Nacional de Artesanías. On the other hand, items here are not as carefully selected, and it may take longer to find something suitable. Bargaining is essential, especially for larger purchases. Besides handicrafts, this market has big selections of low-priced shoes and clothing.

Shoppers who prefer modern comfort, or who are short of time, can stop by the **Metrosur** and **Metrocentro** shopping centres, adjacent to one another on Boulevard Los Héroes across from the Hotel Camino Real. Each has several shops with well selected handicraft items and the added convenience of air conditioning and credit cards, but prices tend to be higher than at the markets, and most of the time there is no bargaining.

Other handicrafts shops are located in the big luxury hotels and along the departure concourse of the international airport. Because there are several shops at the airport, there is some price competition. Prices are higher than in town, but not outrageously so.

■ Art and Books

El Árbol de Dios *(Final Calle La Mascota at Avenida Masferer Sur, Urbanización el Maquilishuat,* ☎ *224-6200)*, literally the tree of God, is an art gallery and restaurant belonging to renowned Salvadoran painter Fernando Llort. Some original paintings and reproductions of some of his works are offered for sale.

There is a scattering of **art galleries** in Colonia San Benito near the *zona rosa* along Calle La Reforma, Avenida Las Palmas and Avenida La Capilla.

Bookmarks *(Boulevard del Hipódromo 520, zona rosa)*, situated in a small shopping centre next to Restaurant Basilea, has a small selection of books and magazines in English.

■ Miscellaneous

Villas Españolas, near the top of Paseo Escalón, is a small shopping centre with exclusive and expensive boutiques.

At the **Metrocentro** and **Metrosur** shopping centres, next to each other on Boulevard Los Héroes across from the Hotel Camino Real, there are gourmet shops where the makings of a good picnic can be assembled. Other shops at these malls offer everyday items of the sort that can be found in cities around the world. Both there and at the small shopping centre next to Restaurant Basilea on Boulevard del Hipódromo in the *zona rosa* are branches of **Shaw's**, known locally for hand-made chocolates and pastries.

For basic food or household items, there is the **Mercado Central**, three blocks south of Calle Rubén Darío between 7ª and 9ª Avenidas Sur in the city centre. The **Mercado Ex-Cuartel**, at Calle Delgado and 8ª Avenida Norte, has inexpensive shoes and clothing.

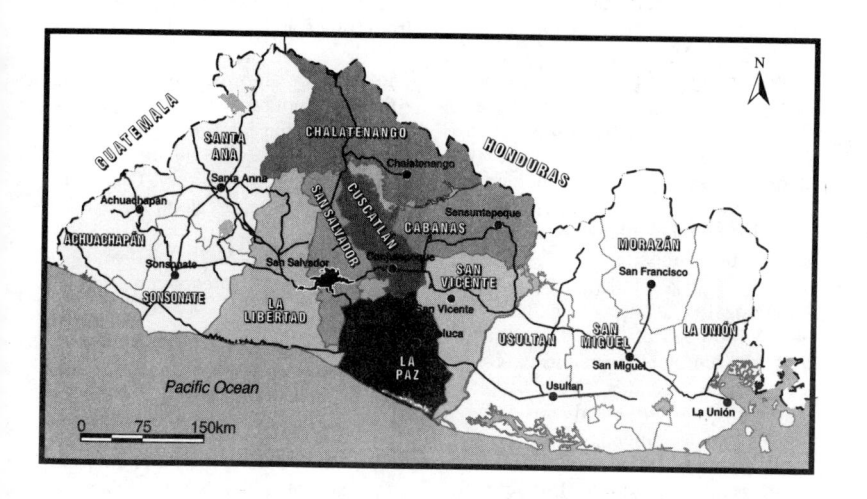

CENTRAL EL SALVADOR

Here we cover the central region of the country minus San Salvador and its immediate surroundings, which are dealt with in the previous chapter. Because El Salvador is so compact, every place mentioned in this chapter is close enough to the capital to be visited on single-day excursions, ranging from the small mountain town of **La Palma** in the north with its profusion of handicrafts to the beaches of the **Costa del Sol** in the south, which many Salvadorans consider to be the finest in the country. This region also includes the colonial charm of **San Vicente**, the bazaar-like atmosphere of **Cojutepeque** and the ancient ruins of **Joya de Cerén** and **San Andrés**.

The proximity of the capital, and the fact that many travellers do return there each night, means that demand for hotels and restaurants in many of these other places remains weak, and consequently even some fair-sized towns are bereft of establishments offering what most visitors would consider acceptable standards, although simple *hospedajes* can be found in most towns. But this is not a problem everywhere: there are good hotels along the coast, and even in La Palma it is possible to find lodgings that are cheerful and pleasant. The sea breezes and the mountain air are preferable to what people have to breathe in San Salvador, and a night or two away from the capital will be an agreeable experience even for the most timid and discerning traveller.

The central zone of El Salvador comprises seven of the country's 14 administrative departments, namely La Libertad, San Salvador, La Paz, Cuscatlán, San Vicente, Cabañas and Chalatenango. The corresponding departmental capitals are Santa Tecla, San Salvador, Zacatecoluca, Cojutepeque, San Vicente, Sensuntepeque and Chalatenango, respectively. The Río Lempa forms a natural boundary between the central and eastern zones.

A suggested itinerary to the "near east," in other words the more easterly part of central El Salvador, starts by leaving San Salvador on the Carretera Panamericana (Pan-American Highway), past Lago de Ilopango, an enticing place to stop for a meal, and on to Cojutepeque to stroll through the streets that form part of a vast bazaar. From atop the Cerro de las Pavas there are splendid views of the surrounding countryside and volcanoes in the distance. Continuing east, the next stop is Ilobasco, noted for its hand-painted ceramic objects, and then it is on to San Vicente, with its delightful colonial atmosphere. A visit to the region might wind up in one of the following ways: return to San Salvador for the night, stay over in San Vicente, push on toward San Miguel in the "far east," or swing south via Zacatecoluca to the beaches of the Costa del Sol and spend the night there, and perhaps a few days of sun and surf.

If beaches are part of your reason for coming to El Salvador, the Costa del Sol (literally, the sun coast) is a good area to linger, although budget travellers may feel squeezed. **La Libertad**, further west along the Pacific coast, is decidedly scruffier and the beaches are less appealing, but lodgings are more affordable and seafood lovers are well looked after. The choice of restaurants makes La Libertad an interesting spot for day trips down from the capital, just a half-hour away.

The ruins of Joya de Cerén and San Andrés are not really as exciting as one might hope, but both lie near the main route between San Salvador and the western part of the country. One or the other is worth a stop along the way.

Last but far from least, La Palma lies amid rugged, pine-forested countryside near the northern fringe of El Salvador. The town is noted mostly for the brightly coloured designs that have spurred an avalanche of handicrafts. It is also a base for mountain hikes and for relaxation in the fresh mountain air. As well, it lies along the route between San Salvador and the Mayan ruins of Copán in Honduras.

Finding Your Way Around

■ By Car

San Salvador is the base for many trips around central El Salvador. As the capital and biggest city in the country, it lies at the heart of the highway network, with roads radiating in several directions.

Most are two-lane highways, but the following have four lanes: the Carretera Panamericana (Pan-American Highway) northwest toward Santa Ana, passing near Los Chorros recreational area and the archeological sites of San Andrés and Joya de Cerén; short stretches of the Carretera Panamericana east to Lago de Ilopango, San Vicente and eastern El Salvador as well as to the cutoff for Ilobasco; and the Autopista del Sur (the southern highway, which in reality goes southeast) to the international airport and to cutoffs for roads to the Costa del Sol and Zacatecoluca.

Other roads of interest include the highway heading west and then south to the coastal resort town of La Libertad, and the Troncal del Norte (northern trunk highway) past the Guazapa volcano to the cutoff for Chalatenango, continuing north to La Palma and to the Honduran border at El Poy, en route to Copán or San Pedro Sula.

In general these highways are in good condition, although the Carretera Panamericana east of San Salvador is rather narrow for the traffic volumes it has to carry, and speeds are slow. Northern portions of the Troncal del Norte are in rough shape, with gaping potholes in some places and the asphalt totally missing in others. This should be taken into account when planning a day excursion to La Palma.

■ **By Bus**

Buses radiate to spots all over the country from San Salvador, with route numbers assigned to nearly all intercity and rural links. Service is very frequent on most routes to and from San Salvador, with departures often just a few minutes apart. One significant exception is the infrequent and slow service to and from the Costa de Sol. Some trips can be slow because of numerous stops and underpowered engines, especially up the mountains to La Palma and El Poy. Because of the frequency of service, there is usually little need to check on schedules. The only reliable way to get schedule information is to go to the terminal and ask a driver or clerk.

From San Salvador

Some places covered in this chapter are served by buses leaving from San Salvador's **Terminal de Oriente** (eastern terminal), located in the east of the city in front of the railway freight sheds near where Avenida Juan Pablo changes names to Boulevard Ejército Nacional. The closest cross street is 38ª Avenida Norte. Here is a partial list of intercity routes leaving from this terminal:
- 110 to San Sebastián
- 111 to Ilobasco
- 113 to Cojutepeque
- 116 to San Vicente
- 119 to La Palma and El Poy
- 125 to Chalatenango

The **Terminal Rutas del Pacífico** (the Pacific or southern terminal) is located on the eastern side of the Autopista Sur on the southern edge of the city. Some buses make a loop through the south of the city before heading back to the highway and out into the countryside. Buses leaving from this terminal include:
- 133 to Zacatecoluca
- 134 to La Herradura, with connections along the way for Route 513 to the Costa del Sol
- 495 direct to the Costa del Sol (infrequent service)

The **Terminal de Occidente** (western terminal) is situated southwest of the city centre near the intersection of Boulevard Venezuela and 49ª Avenida Sur. It is served by taxis and by city bus routes 4, 27 and 34. Buses from here include:
- 102 to La Libertad
- 108 to San Juan Opico, stopping at Joya de Cerén
- 201 to Santa Ana, stopping near Ruinas de San Andrés (look for buses

marked *Ordinario*; those marked *Directo* may not stop).

From Other Towns

In smaller towns there are no formal bus terminals. Buses leave from streets near the public markets or central plazas and can also be caught along the highway at the edge of town.

■ **By Taxi**

For half-day excursions taxis are usually cheaper than car rentals, and even for full-day excursions the price may not be that much higher than for a car, depending on the distance travelled and the time spent in each place. These elements should be set out clearly when negotiating a price. Taxis parked in front of the bigger hotels sometimes charge more than the taxis serving other stands.

★ **Exploring**

■ **Joya de Cerén** ★

The ruins of Joya de Cerén (pronounced KHOY-a-day-say-REN) date from 14 centuries ago. Little of the original structures is visible, but the museum at the entrance to the site makes it worth a visit.

Joya de Cerén *(free admission; Tue to Sun 9 a.m. to 4:30 p.m.)* is situated about 30 km northwest of San Salvador in the valley of the Río Sucio (literally, dirty river) and can be reached by taking the Carretera Panamericana part way to Santa Ana and then the cutoff leading to San Juan Opico. The ruins lie four kilometres north of the highway junction and 10 km south of San Juan Opico, next to a cluster of grain silos near an old steel bridge. By bus, they can be reached directly by Route 108 from the Terminal de Occidente in San Salvador. Coming from Santa Ana, bus 201 (the *Ordinario*, not the *Directo*) drops passengers at the junction for San Juan Opico, from where buses and pickup trucks cover the last few kilometres.

In the third century A.D., a massive eruption of the Ilopango volcano covered a wide area with a layer of lava two to three metres thick, forcing all survivors to flee. For a long period the region was uninhabitable, but gradually new settlers moved in. Then around the year 600 A.D., the Laguna Caldera volcano just two kilometres from Joya de Cerén began to spew hot ash and other volcanic material, burying the village and part of the valley in lava four to six metres thick. This virtually sealed the village in a time capsule, protecting it from the elements and leaving some dwellings and their contents nearly intact.

The site was discovered accidentally in 1976 when bulldozers were excavating earth for the construction of grain silos. Archeologists from the United States marvelled at the state of preservation and at the degree of sophistication of the dwellings, with their floors of baked clay, suggesting that the ancient Maya who inhabited the area achieved a higher standard of living than previously thought. Scarcely any human remains were found.

The museum at the entrance to the archeological site recounts the history of Joya de Cerén and presents examples of pottery, stone tools and other household implements excavated from the site. Only three small structures are on display to visitors. They

Central El Salvador

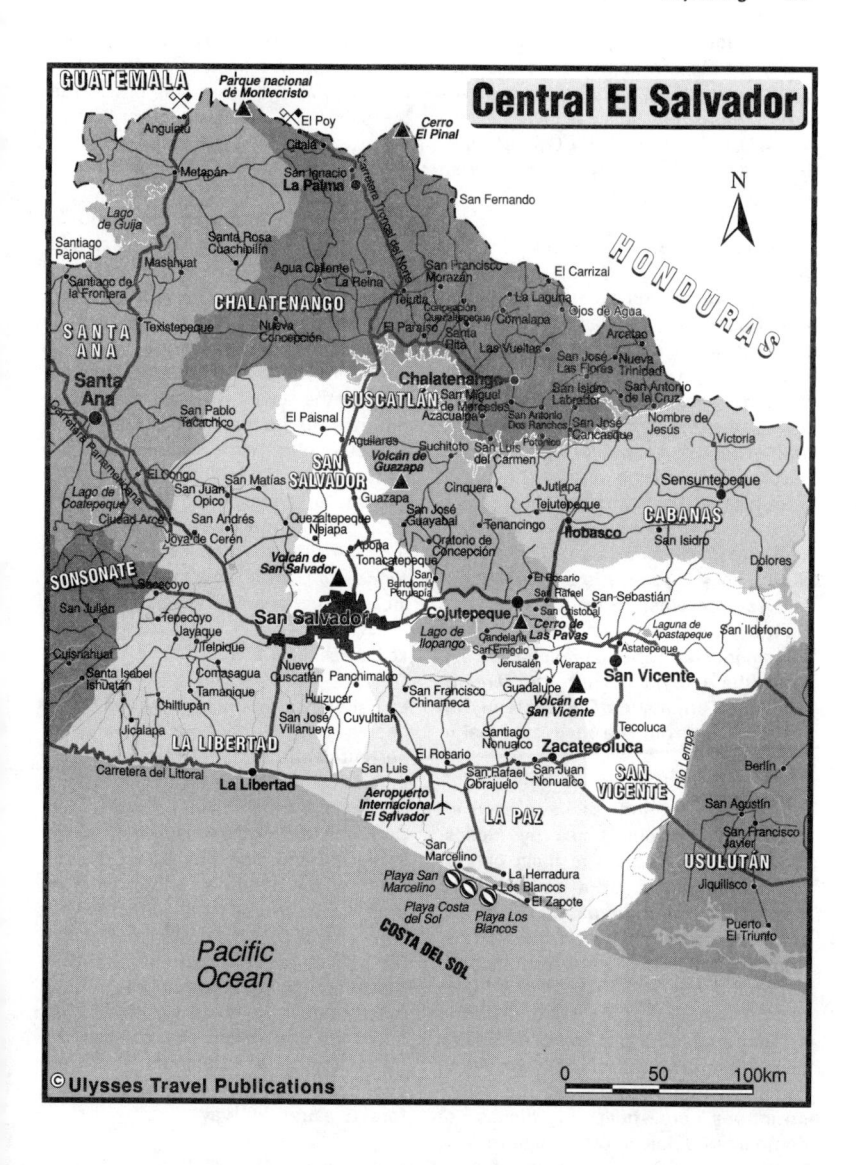

are protected by shelters, and all that is really visible are some low walls that can be viewed from above. An adjacent area is currently being excavated, but work is slowed by a shortage of money. The site is shared with several grain silos.

■ **Ruinas de San Andrés** ★

The San Andrés ruins, sometimes called Las Ruinas de la Campana de San Andrés (*campana* means bell, and the main section of the ruins is bell-shaped), consist mostly of a series of low stone mounds. What makes the site attractive to some visitors is its setting, overlooking a majestic valley with hills visible in the distance.

The site *(free admission; Tue to Sun 9 a.m. to 4:30 p.m.)* is situated about midway between San Salvador and Santa Ana just off the Carretera Panamericana. It can be reached by bus 201 (the *Ordinario*, not the *Directo*) from the Terminal de Occidente in San Salvador or from the main terminal in Santa Ana.

The area is thought to have been inhabited at various times by Pipiles, Mayas and Aztecs. The main part of the site consists of a series of 15 ceremonial mounds dating from the eighth century A.D. and two stone-ringed plazas, one of which faces a pyramid 22 m (72 ft) high and 50 m (164 ft) square at its base. Another structure has four platforms, extending deep underground, which have yet to be excavated. Several of the minor structures are built of blocks of compacted volcanic ash. There may be as many as 200 structures in the area, but so far few have been explored. Grinding stones, pottery shards and other objects from the site were on display at the Museo Nacional in San Salvador (temporarily closed). San Andrés lies five kilometres from Joya de Cerén as the crow flies but further by road.

■ **Chalatenango** ★

This peaceful mountain town 69 km (43 mi) northeast of San Salvador (reached by the Troncal del Norte and then east from a clearly marked junction; bus 125 from the Terminal de Oriente in San Salvador) was an important centre of military activity during the civil war but has now returned to its earlier calm. It is an attractive place with cobbled streets, a picturesque cathedral, a bustling market, a relaxed central plaza, and beautiful mountain scenery all around. Just outside town is the Agua Fría *turicentro* with swimming pools, lockers, gardens and food stalls.

■ **La Palma** ★★★

La Palma is a mountain town of 6,000 people that has become the most important centre of handicraft production in El Salvador. It lies along the Troncal del Norte 81 km (50 mi) north of San Salvador (the highway is in poor shape in places) and nine kilometres (5½ mi) south of the Honduran border crossing at El Poy. It can be reached by the very slow bus 119, which runs hourly from the Terminal de Oriente in San Salvador, taking four hours for the mostly uphill trip to La Palma and 3½ hours for the return. By car the trip takes about half the time. There are beautiful mountain scenes and pine forests along the way.

The town lies at an altitude of 1,100 m (3,609 ft) and has a pleasant, fresh climate. The area around La Palma was hotly contested during the civil war, imposing partial isolation. Even so, the handicrafts industry survived, and it has flourished with the end of the war. There are now several dozen workshops, each employing anywhere from two to 50 workers. Many of these workshops are open to visitors, and a number of them have shops in front where they sell directly to retail customers. Others ship their entire production to San Salvador and to points abroad.

The industry got its start in the 1970s with the development of a style of painting based on bright colours and simple depictions of myriad elements in Salvadoran rural life. Fernando Llort (pronounced yort), El Salvador's best known contemporary painter, was co-founder of an artisans' cooperative called La Semilla de Díos (literally, the seed of God) which has grown enormously, although Llort is no longer directly involved. His designs grace some of the towels and other textiles that are popular with visitors to El Salvador.

Varnished wood objects in various shapes, hand-painted with brightly coloured designs, are the most commonly produced items and have made the town of La Palma famous. These objects come in a bewildering variety, sometimes in the form of jewellery boxes, and each workshop produces its own designs. They may depict anything from animals to peasants' huts, country churches, celestial objects or wild flowers. Some workshops apply these designs to ceramics, leather or cloth.

The town has a picturesque mountain setting. Although its physical appearance is fairly ordinary by Salvadoran standards, the many workshops that have sprung up in the low-slung buildings lining its streets make it a special place to explore.

There seems to be another one at every corner. La Semilla de Díos, the biggest of them, has a big display room in front. In the rear are a large room filled with artisans at work painting their designs onto pieces of wood, and separate rooms for carpentry and varnish work; these can be visited upon request. A couple of art galleries have sprung up, including one displaying original works and reproductions by Alfredo Linares, noted for his naïve paintings. More information is included under Shopping on page 97.

La Palma has a small, cheerful hotel and several restaurants. It can be used as a base for excursions to the nearby mountains, including hiking trips to Cerro El Pital, the highest peak in El Salvador. Guides can also lead visitors to Los Tecomates waterfall or to Río Nunuapa, which is suitable for swimming. Please see the Outdoor Activities section on page 92. Because the surrounding countryside is sparsely populated, wildlife is more abundant than elsewhere in the country. Deer, armadillos, wild hogs and toucans can occasionally be spotted.

Excursions to the fabulous Mayan ruins at **Copán** in Honduras are possible for travellers with cars who are prepared to set out early. The trip takes about four hours in each direction, and it makes the most sense to plan a two-day excursion. Those who are travelling by bus face an all-day journey each way, with connections necessary at El Poy, Nueva Ocotepeque, Santa Rosa de Copán and finally at La Entrada de Copán, turning this, for all practical purposes, into at least a three-day round-trip excursion. There is a bus leaving Santa Rosa at 1 p.m. and arriving in Copán Ruinas at 4 p.m. that avoids the connection at La Entrada. Whether travel is by car or bus, there exists the problem of complying with entry requirements in each country. New visas or tourist cards may be required to re-enter El Salvador. The Honduran embassy in San Salvador is situated at 1ª Calle Poniente 4326, Colonia Escalón (☎ 223-856). There is a Salvadoran consulate in the town of Nueva Ocotepeque on the Honduran side just north of the border. The address is 2ª Avenida Sureste, esquina con 5ª Calle Sureste, Barrio San Andrés.

■ Cojutepeque ★★

This bustling market town, the capital of Cuscatlán department, straddles the Carretera Panamericana 32 km east of San Salvador (bus 113 from the Terminal de Oriente). The highway here is lined with market stalls, many of them selling smoked sausage (*salchicha*), a local specialty.

Cojutepeque (pronounced co-khoo-tay-PAY-kay) is set on a hillside, and the two parallel streets leading up from the **parque central** have been converted to covered bazaars, with stalls all the way along, several of them selling hammocks or pottery. At the top is a picturesque colonial church.

About 15 minutes' walk further up the Cerro de las Pavas (literally, hill of the turkeys) is a shrine to the **Virgen de Fátima** consisting of a small plaster figure set in a grotto just below the peak. This is an important site for pilgrims, and it is strewn with flowers, candles and other religious offerings. May 13, the virgin's feast day, is a time of great religious fervour. The hill provides excellent views over Lago de Ilopango and several distant volcanoes.

■ Ilobasco ★★

This otherwise nondescript town is noted for its production of ceramic objects. Situated 54 km (34 mi) east of San Salvador (bus 111 from the Terminal de Oriente), it is connected to the Carretera Panamericana by a winding seven-kilometre road running north from the village of San Rafael.

Ilobasco has an attractive **parque central**, and several of the nearby streets are dotted with workshops producing hand-painted pottery and ceramic objects of various sorts, including clay plaques and items in the shape of motor vehicles. The quality of work varies greatly from one workshop to another, and some seem hooked on rather garish colours, but with a bit of hunting it is easy to find interesting items at reasonable prices.

■ San Sebastián

This small, somewhat tattered town 51 km (32 mi) east of San Salvador (bus 110 from the Terminal de Oriente), located on a secondary road two kilometres off the Carretera Panamericana, used to be known for its fine weaving and brightly coloured hammocks, but the ravages of war drove away part of its industry. San Sebastián remains a trade centre for the basic fibre used in hammocks and certain types of cloth, but much of the downstream production seems to have shifted elsewhere.

■ San Vicente ★★

This is one of those places that lacks any special point of interest but leaves an agreeable impression anyway. Capital of the department of the same name, it is located 59 km (37 mi) east of San Salvador and 85 km (53 mi) west of San Miguel. The town lies three kilometres south of the Carretera Panamericana. Bus 116 runs frequently from the Terminal de Oriente in San Salvador. There are also buses from San Miguel and from Zacatecoluca.

San Vicente is an old town, founded in 1635 by a group of Spanish settlers. During its long history it has endured earthquakes, Indian insurrections and, in the 1980s, fighting between government troops and rebel forces. It lies in the heart of sugar cane country. Approaching by highway from the west, there are excellent views over the Jiboa valley and what appear to be the twin steeples of San Vicente in the distance. In reality, one of these "steeples" is a high, spindly **clock tower** nearly 40 m (131 ft) tall that dominates the **parque central**. The other is indeed the steeple of the 18th-century **cathedral**. The cathedral is big but rather bare inside, with a brilliant white façade.

The town has a strong colonial flavour, with narrow cobbled streets, several small plazas and many churches, including **Iglesia El Pilar**, two blocks from the *parque central*. This is a long, narrow stone structure with many interior arches and columns along with numerous statues of religious figures. It opens onto an appealing, tree-shaded plaza.

The slopes of the **San Vicente volcano**, also known as Chichontepec and reaching 2,180 m (7,152 ft) above sea level, lie just southwest of the town. A rough dirt road goes most of the way to the summit. Two kilometres south of town is the **Amapulapa turicentro**, with swimming pools, lockers, gardens, snack bars and a small trailer park. On the other side of the Carretera Panamericana, five kilometres (3 mi) further east and then one kilometre (½ mi) north along a side road, is the **Laguna de Apastepeque**, with facilities for swimmers (see also p 90).

■ **Zacatecoluca** ★

This friendly, bustling market town, the capital of La Paz department, lies 57 km (35 mi) southeast of San Salvador (bus 133 from the Terminal Rutas del Pacífico) and 23 km (14 mi) southwest of San Vicente (bus 177). From San Salvador, it is reached by the Autopista del Sur and then the Carretera del Litoral (coastal highway). Although situated well inland, Zacatecoluca (sometimes shortened in casual speech to Zacate, with the accent on the second syllable) lies along the shortest route between eastern El Salvador and the Costa del Sol. For people staying at resort hotels along the Costa del Sol, it is a good place to get a glimpse of day-to-day life in a medium-sized Salvadoran city.

Dominating the centre of town is an enormous church with a triple steeple and a painting of the madonna on the façade of the central steeple. The church has a high vaulted interior with many paintings and sculptures. Nearby is the busy public market. Two kilometres southeast of town is the **Ichanmichen turicentro**, one of the biggest in the country, with swimming pools, lockers, restaurants, snack bars and various sporting facilities.

Parks and Beaches

■ **Parks**

Central El Salvador lacks the national parks and nature reserves found in certain other parts of the country, but it does have several *turicentros*. These are government-run leisure parks offering swimming pools, dressing rooms, restaurants and snack bars set on wooded grounds. The usual opening hours are 8 a.m. to 6 p.m. and admission is $0.60 per person plus $0.60 per vehicle.

The **Agua Fría** *turicentro* lies just outside Chalatenango, **Amapulapa** two kilometres south of San Vicente (served by bus 172), and **Ichanmichen** two kilometres southeast of Zacatecoluca (served by local bus 92).

Two very special *turicentros* are **Costa del Sol**, with direct access to one of the best ocean beaches in El Salvador, and **Apastepeque**, situated on the *laguna* (lake) of the same name, which is suitable for swimming.

The **Costa del Sol** *turicentro* is situated just west of the village of Los Blancos and is a handy way for visitors who are not staying at any of the resort hotels to get beach access, lockers and showers. For directions to the Costa del Sol, see the Beaches section immediately below. The *turicentro* can be reached by bus 495 from the Terminal Rutas del Pacífico in San Salvador.

The **Apastepeque** *turicentro* is situated one kilometre north of the Carretera Panamericana from a cutoff five kilometres east of the junction for San Vicente. The cutoff can be reached by buses 301, 304 or 306 from the Terminal de Oriente in San Salvador.

■ **Beaches**

Costa del Sol ★★★

A series of three beaches, **Playa San Marcelino**, **Playa Costa del Sol** and **Playa Los Blancos**, are known collectively as the Costa del Sol. These are among the finest beaches in El Salvador, with broad expanses of sand stretching many kilometres and marvellous sunsets.

To reach the Costa del Sol from San Salvador, head southeast on the Autopista del Sur, the same road that goes to the international airport. Four kilometres before the airport, there is a cutoff to the left. Stay on that road for six kilometres and then turn right. Follow that road for seven kilometres and then turn right again. After eight kilometres, near the village of **San Marcelino**, the road veers to the left and the ocean becomes visible on the right. This is where the Costa del Sol begins. It can be reached by bus 495 (slow and infrequent service) from the Terminal Rutas del Pacífico (Pacific or Southern Terminal) in San Salvador. The taxi fare from San Salvador is about $30, from the international airport about $15.

The Costa del Sol is situated on a narrow isthmus separated from the rest of the mainland by the **Estero de Jaltepeque** (pronounced khal-tay-PAY-kay). As a result the sand is paler than on many other beaches in El Salvador. It still has a grey colour but not as dark as the volcanic sand found in many other spots. The Jaltepeque estuary is home to a variety of birdlife and extends to the mouth of the Río Lempa.

The beaches face the open sea. Waves are often rough and there is a strong undertow. Swimmers should be very cautious.

The Costa del Sol tends to be quiet at midweek, although things pick up on the weekend and can get quite busy during peak holiday periods. A growing number of foreign tourists are arriving.

Unlike weekend visitors from San Salvador, they stay long enough for hotels to be able to recuperate their costs, and this will undoubtedly lead to new development in the coming years.

Accommodations are mostly in the upper price range. Foreign visitors who arrive at the Costa del Sol with prepaid air-and-hotel packages usually end up paying substantially less than those who book after arriving. Visitors on a tight budget who arrive in El Salvador without prepaid hotel rooms may want to consider staying elsewhere. For day visitors, the *turicentro* one kilometre west of the village of Los Blancos provides good facilities for just $0.60 per person.

A number of excursions are possible and hotels can often help with arrangements. A morning cruise along the Estero de Jaltepeque allows glimpses of varied birdlife. Tours to other regions of El Salvador are offered to visitors who use the Costa del Sol as their base. Day-long tours go on several days of the week from the Tesoro Beach hotel to different spots in western and central El Salvador, including Santa Ana, Cerro Verde national park, San Vicente and Cojutepeque. Even though these tours are usually organized on behalf of particular groups staying at the hotel, anyone is free to join, and prices are reasonable.

One hindrance for visitors who arrive without a car is the paucity of transportation. Bus service to and from the Costa del Sol is infrequent by Salvadoran standards and slow by any measure. The nearest taxi stand is at the international airport and although taxis can be summoned by telephone, this extra distance adds not only to the time (about a half hour) but to the cost as well.

La Libertad ★

This is the nearest beach resort to San Salvador and, as a result, the most popular in the country. The beaches directly in town tend to be rocky and a little on the scruffy side, but there are better beaches on either side of town and a frequent local bus service.

La Libertad lies just 31 km (19 mi) from San Salvador, a little west and then straight south to the coast by a direct highway. A slower but more scenic alternate route goes via the village of Panchimalco (see p 67). La Libertad lies along the Carretera del Litoral (coastal highway), which connects the eastern and western parts of the country. Bus 102 runs frequently from the Terminal de Occidente in San Salvador. Bus 187 runs less often from Comalapa, near the international airport, and bus 287 runs several times daily along the Carretera del Litoral from Sonsonate in the west, a slow but picturesque trip. A local bus, bearing the route number 80, runs frequently between El Sunzal in the west and Playa San Diego to the east of La Libertad. There are also local taxis.

Facing the beach near the centre of town is a cluster of appealing restaurants specializing in fresh fish and seafood. La Libertad is more popular as a day resort and accommodations do not meet very high standards, although there is a reasonable selection.

La Libertad is also a fishing port. At the main pier visitors can watch fishing boats being winched from the sea in what amounts to something of a show as it has to be timed to catch the waves.

Several hotels and beach clubs offer pools, changing rooms and other facilities for the use of day visitors. Among these is a beach club called **Fishermen's El Salvador** facing Playa Las Flores one kilometre east of town *($3 Tue to Fri, $6 Sat and Sun, closed Mon)*, providing access to a sandy beach, three pools, lounge chairs, changing rooms, showers, a bar and a restaurant. **Hotel Malecón de Don Lito** (not to be confused with other hotels bearing Don Lito in their names) faces Playa La Paz on the eastern side of town *($2 every day)* and offers access to a rocky beach and a big kidney-shaped pool.

Playa El Sunzal lies eight kilometres west of La Libertad below the Carretera del Litoral (served by local bus 80) but does not have direct road access. Some surfers consider this to be one of the finest surfing beaches in the world, and even during the height of the war in the 1980s some young American surfers found their way here, apparently oblivious to what was going on elsewhere in the country. The road runs along a ridge high above the beach, which can be reached by a footpath or by a small side road to the adjacent **Playa El Tunco** just to the east. Playa El Sunzal is undeveloped, whereas there are several pleasant and inexpensive restaurants along Playa El Tunco. Both are broad and sandy.

Further east and closer to town lie **Playa El Majahual**, **Playa San Blas** and **Playa Conchalío**, all sandy but a little on the scruffy side. Playa Conchalío has several small restaurants. **Playa La Paz** faces the centre of town but is quite rocky, especially toward the eastern side. There are several very good restaurants on the western side of this beach and a number of more modest establishments on the eastern side.

Further east lie **Playa Las Flores** and **Playa San Diego**, which are broader, sandier and more appealing. Playa San Diego is reached by a side road which branches from the highway east of La Libertad.

Outdoor Activities

Hiking

The mountainous countryside around **La Palma** offers a variety of hiking opportunities, including the ascent of **Cerro El Pital**, which at 2,730 m (8,957 ft) above sea level is the highest peak in El Salvador. It is not a volcanic peak and as such lacks the characteristic conical shape. From the top climbers can peer into Honduras just two kilometres away. To reach Cerro El Pital, go first to San Ignacio, four kilometres north of La Palma (bus 119, hourly). From there a four-wheel drive vehicle goes two or three times a day to the high village of Río Chiquito ($1 fare), and then the climb is about one hour by foot along an unmarked trail. **Miramundo**, a lower peak at 2,100 m (6,890 ft) but with stunning views over a wide area, can be climbed in about 90 minutes from Río Chiquito. By prior arrangement, transport can be provided directly from La Palma to Río Chiquito. For groups, a four-wheel-drive vehicle and guide cost about $50 a day. Inquire at Hotel La Palma near the entrance to the town *(☎ 335-9012)*.

From La Palma itself, **Río Nunuapa** (meaning silent in the Nahua language) is a clean mountain stream suitable for swimming, and can be reached by foot in about 40 minutes. Another hike can take visitors to **Los Tecomates** waterfall, 90 minutes away by foot. For either of these excursions, a guide is needed to show the way. Again, information is available at Hotel La Palma.

Closer to San Salvador, the slopes of the **Guazapa** volcano, which reaches a mere 1,420 m (4,659 ft) above sea level, obtained a certain notoriety in the early 1980s as a dumping ground for the corpses of political and social activists who were murdered as a warning to others by the country's nefarious right-wing death squads. The area was also a base for actions by FMLN guerrillas. To reach the volcano, go first to the town of Guazapa along the Troncal del Norte (northern trunk road) about 25 km (15½ mi) north of San Salvador (bus 119 or 125 from the Terminal de Oriente). From there a dirt road runs three kilometres (2 mi) east to the village of Nance Verde. Pickup trucks from the market in Guazapa occasionally travel this road; otherwise it is about a half-hour by foot. It takes about an hour by foot to climb to the summit from Nance Verde along an unmarked trail.

Swimming and Boating

The beaches of the Costa del Sol and La Libertad provide opportunities for swimming, but everyone should beware of a dangerous undertow. The **Laguna de Apastepeque** northeast of San Vicente (see p 90) and **Río Nunuapa** near La Palma (see above) offer lake and river swimming respectively. Boat trips along the **Estero de Jaltepeque** can be arranged from the Costa del Sol. Inquire at local hotels for information.

Bicycling

Cycling the 81 km (50 mi) from San Salvador to La Palma requires a sturdy pair of legs because of long climbs along poorly paved northern portions, but it can be done. Traffic, fairly dense leaving San Salvador, becomes progressively lighter further north, where the scenery is very rewarding. The 31 km (19 mi) from San Salvador to La Libertad is a fairly easy jaunt, but there are long climbs on the way back, and on weekends and holidays traffic can be quite dense. When cycling in San Salvador and its outskirts, it is wise to follow the example of some local cyclists and to use a mask that covers the mouth and nose as protection against exhaust from poorly adjusted diesel engines. Further east, roads between San Vicente, Zacatecoluca and the Costa del Sol are flat, well paved and lightly travelled, but the scenery is less interesting and there have been reports of banditry near Tecoluca, midway between San Vicente and Zacatecoluca.

Accommodation

Rudimentary hotels called *hospedajes* can be found in all towns mentioned in this section, with prices usually under $5 a night, but in most cases standards are very low, with dark, prison-like rooms. The more acceptable hotels are mentioned below.

■ **La Palma**

Hotel La Palma *($18 in some rooms, $23 in three-bed rooms; along the main road at the entrance to town,* ☎ *335-012)* is a friendly, cheerful place offering five simple, attractive rooms with tile floors, wood ceilings and terraces with comfortable wooden armchairs. Rooms face a pretty garden, which still needs a bit of work, and mountains are visible beyond. Snacks and light meals are available. The hotel has been around since 1942, but it closed in 1980 because of the war. It reopened in 1994.

Behind the market lie the air-conditioned Restaurant El Paraíso and two very basic *hospedajes* with dark rooms for $3 a night.

■ **San Vicente**

Hotel Villas Españolas *($12; Avenida José María Cornejo 12 behind the cathedral,* ☎ *333-322)* is a new hotel two blocks from the *parque central*. Its 17 rooms are set along an ugly driveway but are reasonably presentable inside. Some have television, and all have fans.

Hotel Central, facing the *parque central*, is cheaper and more rudimentary.

■ **Costa del Sol**

Tony's Inn *($6; in the village of Los Blancos, no phone)* offers rudimentary lodgings in a series of eight small *cabañas* with fan. Toilet and shower facilities are shared and rather primitive. Unfortunately, this is about the best that is available for travellers who are not prepared to splurge in one of the resort hotels.

Hotel Pacific Paradise *($60, VI - MC - AE - DC;* ≡, ≈, ℜ, *bar; 6 km east of Los Blancos,* ☎ *334-0601,* ⇄ *in San Salvador 287-0545)* has 50 rooms including four suites at $89 accommodating up to six people. A well-shaded area lies between the beach and the hotel, which is owned by a company controlled by the Salvadoran military. The hotel itself is rather run down, but its pleasant open-air restaurant has the best food on the Costa del Sol.

Hotel Izalco Cabaña Club *($62 including service, $14 supplement during peak holiday periods, AE;* ≡, ≈, ℜ, *bar; 1 km west of Los Blancos,* ☎ *in San Salvador 223-764,* ⇄ *224-363)* offers 22 big, comfortable rooms. Right in front is a broad, sandy beach.

Tesoro Beach Hotel And Country Club *($152, VI - MC - AE - DC;* ≡, *tv,* ≈, ℜ, *bar, tennis, 9-hole golf course; 3 km east of Los Blancos,* ☎ *and* ⇄ *334-0600)* is the most lavish resort hotel in El Salvador. It has a vast but appealing lobby with a lofty, arched wooden ceiling, a colourful mural covering one wall, and comfortable armchairs beneath. The V-shaped building has 120 rooms set in two-story wings on either side of a central pavilion. Between the hotel and a broad sandy beach are pools and a series of pleasant outdoor dining areas. Meals are served buffet-style on weekends and holidays, *à la carte* during quieter periods. The hotel opened just before the onset of the civil war, and it took great financial heroism to keep it open throughout.

■ **La Libertad**

West of La Libertad

Cabañas Don Chepe *($7* ⊗, *$15* ≡; ≈; *Playa Conchalío,* ☎ *335-3333)* has pleasant grounds, but most of its 11 rooms are tiny and cell-like. The upstairs rooms, which are air-conditioned, are bigger but rather bare. The beach lies several minutes' walk away.

Hotel Conchalío, almost next door, is similar. There are several small restaurants nearby.

Centro El Bosque *($12-$18; near Playa El Tunco, 1 km north of the highway)* is an unusual spot situated in a heavily wooded area reached by a rough stone road running north from the Carretera del Litoral about six kilometres west of La Libertad. It consists of six very crude *cabañas* set in the woods next to a big pool and small restaurant, with a muddy lake nearby.

Hotel El Pacífico *($16; pool, restaurant; Playa El Majahual)* has tiny, crudely furnished rooms and loud music blaring much of the time. The beach is close by.

Hotel Los Arcos *($23, VI - MC - AE - DC; ≡, tv, ≈, ℜ, bar; Playa Conchalío, ☎ 335-3490)* is situated just a few hundred metres west of La Libertad, about five minutes' walk from the beach. It has 20 large rooms with tile floors and rather ordinary decor. Rooms are set around a pool and small garden. The dining room is big but a little dark.

In Town

Hotel Porto Bello *($5-$6; 1ª Avenida Sur at 2ª Calle Poniente in the centre of La Libertad, ☎ 335-3013)* is a dark, foreboding place that feels more like an Institution than a hotel. It has 20 rooms.

La Posada de Don Lito *($42, VI - MC - AE - DC; ≡, ≈, ℜ, bar; facing Playa La Paz on the western side of La Libertad, ☎ 335-3166)* incorporates the next-door Posada de Don Rodrigo as well. Together they have 20 rooms that are decorated haphazardly at best, but there are pleasant terraces in front. The beach is rather rocky and lies close by; there are some surfers. The hotel has two small pools and a beachfront restaurant.

Hotel Malecón de Don Lito *($42, VI - MC - AE - DC; ≡, ≈; facing Playa La Paz on the eastern side of La Libertad, ☎ 335-3201)* has 16 rooms that show the same dismal taste in furnishing as the hotel's namesake on the western side of town. The terraces in front of the rooms have hammocks and wooden armchairs, and they face a kidney-shaped pool. The beach in front is palm-shaded but very rocky.

East of La Libertad

Three small hotels line Playa San Diego. With their isolated locations and lack of evening restaurant service, they are not suitable for visitors without cars. They are **Villas de San Diego** *($26 for up to four people, $35 on weekends; ☎ 335-3320)*, with six very plain rooms and a sunny pool; **Villa del Pacífico** *($29; ≡, ≈, restaurant closing at 6 p.m., ☎ 335-3334)*, with five small, simple, bare rooms; and **Hotel Las Cabañas de Don Lito** *($46, VI - MC - AE - DC; ≈, ≈, restaurant open for breakfast and lunch only)*, with three rooms displaying Don Lito's bizarre taste in decoration, landscaped grounds, a pool with shaded terrace, and the beach a few minutes' walk away.

☒ Restaurants

All towns mentioned in this section have restaurants of some sort, but in most cases they are very simple and not really worthy of mention. Below are suggested restaurants in all towns and resort areas for which we have provided hotel recommendations.

■ Chalatenango

Restaurant El Paraíso *(11 a.m. to 11 p.m., behind the market)* is an air conditioned spot with meats and sandwiches on the menu.

■ La Palma

Cafeteria La Terraza *(9 a.m. to 9 p.m., near the central plaza)* is pleasant and very inexpensive, with an upstairs terrace reached by a treacherous spiral stairway. It offers sandwiches, chicken, steak, soups and a variety of fruit drinks.

Almost next door is **Cafetería La Estancia** *(8:30 a.m. to 8 p.m.)* with a comparable menu and a small, very ordinary ground-floor dining room.

■ San Vicente

Restaurant Central and **Restaurant Taiwan**, both facing the *parque central*, offer a variety of meat dishes, soups and sandwiches. Restaurant Taiwan also has some Chinese dishes. Both are very inexpensive.

■ Costa del Sol

Hotel restaurants are really the only sure bets here. The best is at the **Hotel Pacific Paradise**, six kilometres (4 mi) east of the village of Los Blancos. Food is also good at the **Tesoro Beach**, three kilometres (2 mi) east of Los Blancos. A variety of meat, fish and seafood dishes are offered on pleasant, breezy open-air terraces, served buffet-style weekends and holidays (which means more food but less selection than ordering *à la carte*). Count on spending $6 to $10 for main courses or $12 for a full buffet.

■ La Libertad

A cluster of pleasant, open-air restaurants line the western part of Playa La Paz near the centre of La Libertad. **Restaurant Sandra, Restaurant Rancho Mar El Delfín** and **Restaurant Punta Roca** all have friendly service, fresh ingredients and tablecloths. The Punta Roca has an upstairs terrace. Seafood cocktails run at $3 to $6, seafood soups $6 to $8, fresh fish $5 to $7, shrimp dishes $6 to $8, and lobster $8 to $10. Meat dishes, rice dishes and sandwiches are also available.

Restaurant Camino Real *(7 a.m. to 8 p.m., at the northern entrance to La Libertad)* is a vast, very inexpensive self-service emporium with seating at long tables. It goes light on the meat and offers a good selection of traditional Salvadoran dishes, including superb cornmeal *tamales*.

At Playa El Tunco, there are several pleasant and inexpensive restaurants, including **La Bocana** and **Juanita**, emphasizing fresh fish and seafood. There are many small and simple restaurants along Playa El Majahual and Playa Conchalío, and two or three more elaborate spots along Playa San Diego.

Entertainment

There is little by way of evening entertainment in the region covered by this chapter. At the Tesoro Beach hotel on the Costa del Sol, some evening activities are planned for foreign visitors.

💲 Shopping

■ La Palma

La Palma has become something of a mecca for shoppers seeking original handicrafts (*artesanías* in Spanish). Although a great variety of items can be found in San Salvador, La Palma is where many of them are produced, and it is possible to visit the workshops, which are scattered around the centre of the town. Street names are not used much in La Palma, and people are more likely to know a particular *taller* (pronounced ta-YEHR and meaning workshop) than the street on which it is situated.

The best known is **La Semilla de Dios**, co-founded in the 1970s by Salvadoran painter Fernando Llort (pronounced yort), where visitors can buy — and observe the production of — brightly coloured hand-painted wooden objects depicting aspects of rural life that have made the fame of La Palma. Numerous other workshops produce similar items, in various shapes and sizes, though on a smaller scale. Other workshops include **Los Cipreses**, **El Yute**, **El Pinabete**, **San Silvestre**, **San Antonio**, **Artesanías La Palma**, **El Jarrón** and **Los Pinares**. Some of them produce only wooden objects, while others turn out brightly coloured objects using leather, cloth, pottery or metal as their medium.

Probably the best approach for visitors is simply to set off on foot and stroll through the streets of this compact town, stopping to poke in wherever they spot something that looks interesting. Besides the handicrafts workshops, there is the **Galería de Arte Alfredo Linares**, where Linares, one of El Salvador's better known painters, presents original works and reproductions. His style is quite different from Llort's, but like Llort he leans toward the naive.

■ Ilobasco

Ilobasco has become known for hand-painted ceramic objects, some tinted in rather garish shades. As in La Palma, streets in the centre of town are dotted with small workshops. Many sell elaborately decorated clay plaques or ceramic items shaped like animals, motor vehicles or other objects, some of them quite fanciful. The quality of work varies from one workshop to the next, and it is worth looking around. Prices are often cheaper than in San Salvador.

■ Cojutepeque

At the sprawling market in **Cojutepeque**, visitors can find locally made pottery and hammocks. Stalls along the highway sell smoked sausages, a local specialty.

Elsewhere, shopping is more limited. The Tesoro Beach hotel on the Costa del Sol has a gift shop selling items from several parts of El Salvador, including the famous beach towels with their intricate designs, some of them inspired by paintings from La Palma.

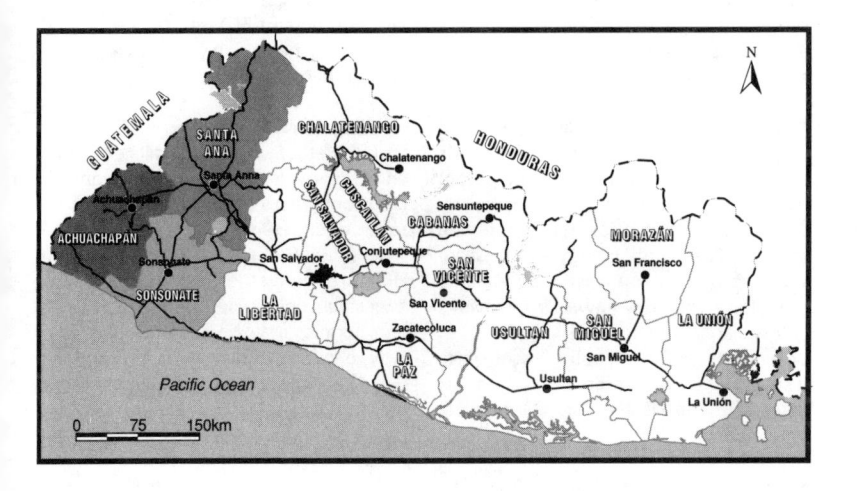

WESTERN EL SALVADOR

The western region of El Salvador is a land of verdant coffee plantations and fine mountain vistas, of charming colonial towns and dramatic volcanoes. It also contains the country's only cloud forest, two large and scenic lakes plus several smaller ones, four official border crossings with Guatemala and one of Central America's seediest seaports. Beaches in the area are undeveloped and offer few amenities.

The western departments of Santa Ana, Sonsonate and Ahuachapán are each anchored by a departmental capital of the same name. Among the three, only Santa Ana is really attractive to tourists. There are, however, plenty of smaller towns that are well worth seeing. Although western El Salvador was spared heavy fighting in the 1980s, it could not escape some of the indirect effects that were felt across the entire country, notably in the neglect of economic development.

Because the war kept most tourists away for 12 years, and because most places of interest to tourists or business travellers are within easy striking distance of San Salvador, the region has only a few hotels offering the levels of comfort or charm that many visitors will be looking for. Santa Ana, Metapán and Ahuachapán each have hotels that are reasonably pleasant. There are attractive places to stay along the shore of Lago de Coatepeque, a landmark hotel in Cerro Verde national park facing the Izalco volcano, and a lovely mountain inn in the coffee-growing country of

Apaneca. Accommodations tend to be rather basic in the other large towns and next to non-existent in most of the smaller towns.

A tour of western El Salvador could begin in Santa Ana, with visits to its colonial plazas and churches. From there you can head up to Lago de Coatepeque, with its fine mountain setting. The climb continues to Cerro Verde, a national park where a walking trail offers splendid views of the valleys below and spectacular glimpses of volcanoes. For really energetic travellers, Cerro Verde is a base for hikes to the Izalco or Santa Ana volcanoes.

Heading back via Santa Ana (or, alternately, taking a more direct southerly route), you come to Sonsonate, a bustling market town with several colonial churches but little else of real interest. The mountain highway between Santa Ana and Sonsonate is highly scenic, with coffee growing as far as the eye can see and rows of shade trees planted in crazy-quilt patterns on the hillsides. From Sonsonate it is a short hop east to Izalco with its colonial streets and churches. Doubling back and heading north, you reach Nahuizalco, one of the few places in El Salvador where Indian dress is still worn by some of the townspeople. This town is also noted for its production of elaborate wickerwork and rattan furniture. Continuing north through coffee country, you pass the colonial towns of Juayúa and Apaneca. From this area you can make side trips to several smaller towns and to Laguna Verde, a mountain lake surrounded by luxuriant vegetation. Near Ahuachapán you can visit fields with puddles of boiling mud and plumes of steam rising from volcanic vents. Returning east toward Santa Ana, you come to Chalchuapa and the ruins of El Tazumal, entombed in concrete by misguided conservationists.

Heading north from Santa Ana, you reach Metapán, an old hillside town and departure point for excursions to the Montecristo cloud forest and nature reserve, situated in the mountain area where El Salvador, Guatemala and Honduras converge. The reserve is fully accessible only at certain times of year, and permits may be required. On your way back, you can stop at Lago de Güija, a large, tranquil body of water that extends into Guatemala. Ancient stone carvings have been found on an island in the lake.

That, in a nutshell, covers the main attractions in western El Salvador. On the Pacific coast, you can visit the port of Acajutla, but it is a rather dismal place. Probably the best beaches in the area are found at Barra de Santiago, further west, but access is poor and facilities are primitive. If you go, plan on a day visit rather than on staying overnight.

Finding Your Way Around

■ By Car

Highways in the western part of El Salvador are the best in the country and seem to be kept in better shape than the potholed roads of eastern El Salvador. The **Carretera Panamericana** (Pan-American Highway) is four lanes wide from San Salvador to Santa Ana. Further west it narrows to two lanes, continuing to Ahuachapán and onward to Las Chinamas, the busiest of the border crossings with Guatemala and a likely port of entry for travellers arriving from Guatemala City.

Another highway runs northwest from Santa Ana to an alternate border crossing at San Cristóbal. Roads also run southwest from Santa Ana to Sonsonate (a very scenic road through coffee-growing country) and north to Metapán and Anguiatú, yet another border point (where travellers arrive when coming from Chiquimula or Esquipulas). The fourth, and most southerly, crossing into Guatemala is at La Hachadura, lying along the so-called **Carretera del Litoral** (coastal highway), essentially an inland highway running parallel to the coast. Further east it runs closer to the coast and becomes a very hilly and winding route.

Sonsonate is another important crossroads of the highway system with roads running east to San Salvador, south to the coast at Acajutla (a few kilometres after it meets the coastal highway), northeast to Santa Ana, and northwest to Ahuachapán (along another scenic route through coffee country).

Fear of crime has kept most highways almost devoid of traffic at night in recent times. You would be wise to restrict your travelling to daylight hours. Wandering livestock and disabled vehicles parked along unlighted stretches of highway provide additional reasons for avoiding night driving. Although the border crossings stay open at night, they see little activity after about 7 p.m.

■ **By Bus**

Buses run so frequently along the busier intercity routes that waiting times are shorter than on urban routes in many North American cities. The problem, as elsewhere in the country, is with crowded conditions and low average speeds because of the many stops the buses make. Service ends shortly after dusk. Virtually all buses have route numbers, which are painted on the front and rear of each vehicle. There are no printed timetables. Accurate information on departure times is available only at the terminals.

On the San Salvador–Santa Ana (Route 201) and San Salvador–Santa Ana–Ahuachapán (Route 205) runs, there are many buses marked *Directo* that make fewer stops. Most San Salvador–Santa–Ana–Ahuachapán buses (Route 202) make only limited stops between San Salvador and Santa Ana.

Santa Ana

Santa Ana has bus connections to many points in the region. Here is a partial listing:

- 201 to San Salvador
- 202 to Ahuachapán
- 220 to Lago de Coatepeque
- 248 to Cerro Verde
- 216 to Sonsonate
- 235 to Metapán

Santa Ana also has **international service** to and from Guatemala City. All services originate in San Salvador, but usually a section of seats is reserved for passengers boarding in Santa Ana. Many of these vehicles are superannuated Greyhound buses, minus the air conditioning and toilets, but in terms of comfort they are superior to the buses operating on routes within El Salvador. The international buses depart from a terminal on 25ª Calle Oriente near 8ª Avenida, not far from the Hotel Internacional.

Western El Salvador

Sonsonate

Local buses go to Izalco and Nahuizalco. There are also bus connections to many points in the region. Here is a partial listing:

- 249 to Nahuizalco, Apaneca and Ahuachapán
- 216 to Santa Ana
- 252 to Acajutla

less frequent service on:
- 257 to Playa Los Cóbanos
- 249-B to Playa Metalío
- 287 to La Libertad (along coast)

Ahuachapán

Occasional service is provided on Route 285 from Ahuachapán to Barra de Santiago.

■ By Rail

The only official passenger train in El Salvador runs once daily between Sonsonate and the town of Armenia to the east. Passenger service is also provided, unofficially, by freight trains running between Texistepeque, north of Santa Ana, and Aguilares, which lies north of San Salvador on the road to Chalatenango department. This latter route, not duplicated by any direct highway link, offers interesting scenery in the Río Lempa valley. No fare is collected, and travel is strictly at the rider's risk.

For information:
Ferrocarriles Nacionales de El Salvador
(Salvadoran National Railways)
San Salvador
☎ 271-5632.

■ By Taxi

Taxis may be hired at Santa Ana or Sonsonate for trips around the region. The taxi stand at the central plaza in Santa Ana is recommended. Be sure to advise the driver of your itinerary and how much time you expect to spend at each place, and agree on a price beforehand. For half-day excursions this will be cheaper than renting a car, and even for full-day excursions it may end up costing only slightly more.

In any event, there are no car rental agencies in western El Salvador. At Ahuachapán there are no taxis either, but pickup trucks based at the market provide taxi service.

★ Exploring

■ Santa Ana ★★

This is the second largest city El Salvador. It flourished in the latter half of the 19th century as the coffee boom invigorated the economy of the surrounding area. The proximity of San Salvador (65 km away, less than one hour by car, slightly more by bus), has overshadowed Santa Ana's recent development, leaving the city with a surprisingly rustic atmosphere despite its size (population 260,000). Nonetheless, it is an important regional centre, and although its own attractions are somewhat limited it makes a good jumping-off point for visits to other parts of western El Salvador.

As in much of Central America, most streets and avenues in Santa Ana have numbers rather than names, with numbers rising according to the distance from the central plaza, followed by a cardinal point of the compass relative to that plaza.

Exploring 103

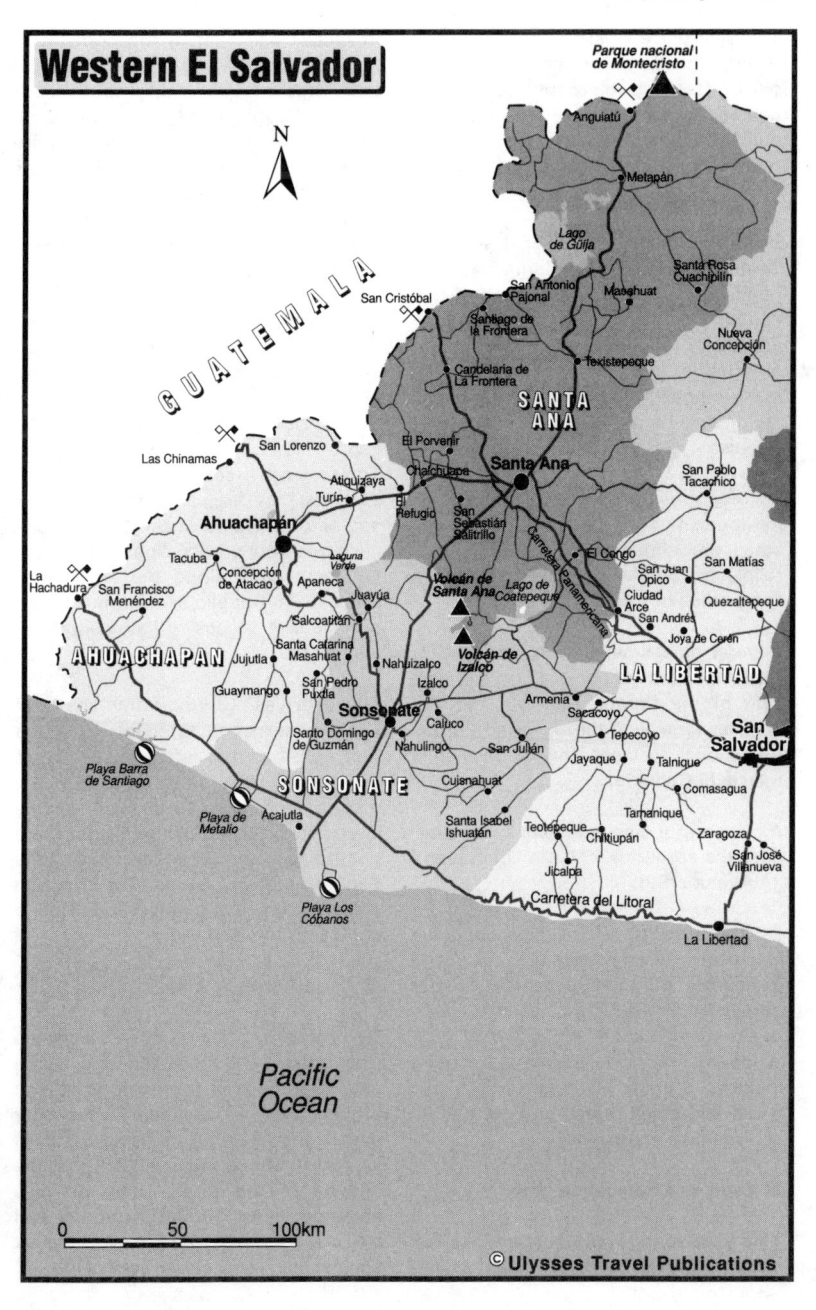

Western El Salvador

The best place to start a visit to Santa Ana is the **Parque Central**, or central plaza. This is a pleasant, tree-shaded square bordered by several historical buildings that have been freshly restored to something approaching their former glory.

Both the **Palacio Municipal** and the **Teatro Nacional de Santa Ana**, a handsome neoclassical turn-of-the-century theatre, have appealing yellow-and-white façades, and are worth entering if you get the chance. The most imposing building in the city, also facing the Parque Central, is the vast Spanish Gothic Revival **cathedral** *(closed 12:30 p.m. to 2:30 p.m.)*, with its lofty spires and intricate carvings on its reddish stone façade. There is a small gift shop at the entrance with religious items and many pigeons on the terrace in front.

Several blocks west (for purposes of reference, the cathedral is on the east side of the Parque Central), there is another appealing plaza, called Parque Menéndez. It faces the colonial-style **Iglesia El Calvario**.

Also worth a visit is **Iglesia El Carmen**, near the corner of 7ª Calle Oriente and 1ª Avenida Sur.

On the outskirts of the city along the Carretera Panamericana is the **Turicentro Sihuatehuacán** *($0.60 per person plus $0.60 per vehicle; open every day 8 a.m. to 6 p.m.)* with wooded grounds, swimming pools, lockers, a roller skating rink, picnic areas and small restaurants. It can be crowded on weekends.

■ Lago de Coatepeque ★★

This vast spring-fed mountain lake lies in the shadow of several volcanoes and in fact is itself set in the crater of a huge former volcano. Heavily wooded land rises steeply from the sides of Lago de Coatepeque (pronounced kwa-tay-PAY-kay), and there are superb views both from the road that rings part of the lake and, much higher up, from the road leading to nearby Cerro Verde. Most of the surrounding area is heavily wooded.

Swimming and boating are popular pastimes here, but many people go simply to enjoy the peaceful atmosphere, sometimes over lunch at the lakeside restaurants of the Hotel del Lago (see p 112) or the Hotel Torremolinos (see p 113). Beaches, such as they are, tend to be narrow and scruffy. Some of the terraces and piers are more appealing. The many private estates along the shore may seem to limit public access, but hotels provide lake access to day visitors for a small fee.

The lake lies 13 km (8 mi) south of Santa Ana. As you approach, avoid the first cutoff to the left, which can be treacherous. It is safer to go the long way around and do a loop at the intersection further along. To get there without a car, take Bus 220 from Santa Ana. If you are coming from San Salvador, you can connect at El Congo and catch the 220 there.

■ Cerro Verde ★★★

Cerro Verde is one of three volcanoes (the other two are Izalco and Santa Ana) that together form a ridge of high ground over which their cones soar even higher. Santa Ana, rising 2,365 m (7,759 ft) above sea level, is by far the highest of the three. They all give stunning views both from above and below. One of the most spectacular—and easily accessible—of these views is found in the Parque Nacional de Cerro Verde (literally, green hill): an unimpeded sight of **Izalco volcano** across a valley from the same height as its naked black cone. For more information on the park, see p 109.

■ Sonsonate

This city of 90,000 people is a hot, noisy, bustling market town, with Sunday the busiest day. It is a rather scruffy place, with little of interest for most tourists. Some of the smaller neighbouring towns are more appealing. The best time to come is during Holy Week, immediately before Easter, when there are many processions and celebrations.

Sonsonate prospered during colonial times, when many churches and convents were erected. The **cathedral** is notable for its 17 different-sized cupolas, intended to help distribute weight and make the structure more resistant to earthquakes.

Iglesia Nuestra Señora del Pilar has a carved baroque façade, and **Iglesia Parroquial** is also imposing. All are clustered within two blocks of the Parque Central.

The small and unimposing colonial church in **San Antonio del Monte**, a district at the western edge of town, has a statue of San Antonio that is thought to have miraculous powers; it draws many pilgrims.

■ Izalco ★

The centre of Izalco (six kilometres (4 mi) east of Sonsonate, reachable by local bus) is bounded by two churches sitting a few blocks apart. In between are a lively small-town market spilling out into the neighbouring streets and many low-slung colonial-style buildings with traditional red-tile roofs. Some of the streets are paved in stone.

Iglesia Dolores, with its impressive hardwood ceiling, is being restored according to the original plans; it looks out onto a small and desolate park. **Iglesia Asunción**, at the other end, is rather homely but faces a more pleasing park. It is flanked by a bell tower that is all that remains of an older church.

On the outskirts of Izalco is the **Turicentro Atecozol** *($0.60 per person plus $0.60 per vehicle; open every day 8 a.m. to 6 p.m.)*, a recreational area with attractive wooded grounds, swimming pools, lockers, small restaurants, picnic areas, and monuments to the Indian gods Tlaloc and Atlacatl.

■ Acajutla and the Western Coast

Acajutla, 20 km (12 mi) southwest of Sonsonate (Bus 252), is a dumpy, seedy commercial seaport with little to recommend it apart from a small handful of seafood restaurants. The beach is dirty and rough, and the whole place has a generally unsavoury atmosphere. It has several small, generally unappealing hotels and a number of brothels.

Barra de Santiago, on the Pacific coast toward the Guatemalan border, offers the best beaches in western El Salvador, on a ribbon of land lying next to a mangrove-lined estuary. Eating and sleeping facilities are quite primitive.

Playa de Metalío and **Playa Los Cóbanos** are situated on either side of the port city of **Acajutla**. They are less attractive. For more information, see p 111.

In earlier times the coastal area east of Acajutla was known as the **Costa del Bálsamo** (Balsam Coast) because of the profusion of balsam trees growing there. Balsam resins were found to have many medicinal applications. Even today they are used in shampoos, cough remedies and a variety of pharmaceutical products. For centuries balsam was a big source of income, with many shipments going to Europe, but now it is extracted on a much smaller scale. The industry remains alive in the area around the largely Indian town of **Cuisnahuat** (situated well inland, reached by a rough road running southeast from Sonsonate, Bus 219). There are caves and waterfalls nearby. The main trading centre for balsam is **San Julián**, just to the north.

■ **North and West of Sonsonate** ★★

The triangle formed by Sonsonate, Santa Ana and Ahuachapán lies in the very heart of El Salvador's coffee country. Rich volcanic soils and shaded mountain slopes provide ideal growing conditions. Shade trees form zigzag patterns up and down the lush hillsides and valleys, and between September and November the coffee beans turn bright red, creating a blaze of colour. The area is dotted with *beneficios*, the industrial plants where the coffee beans are processed. For many years world coffee prices were depressed, leading to an absence of investment in the region. In 1994 prices soared, at least temporarily, giving the area's economy a short-term boost.

Santo Domingo de Guzmán ★

This town, situated eight kilometres (5 mi) west of Sonsonate (Bus 246), is noted for the production of *comales*, the simple grills used to prepare tortillas and a fixture in most Salvadoran kitchens. Within walking distance of the town are a group of three waterfalls, El Escuco, Tepechapa and La Quebrada. (Santo Domingo is also linked to Salcoatitán, further north, by a long and rough road.)

Nahuizalco ★★

The highway between Sonsonate and Ahuachapán weaves its way not only through beautiful countryside but also through several picturesque colonial towns. The first of these is Nahuizalco, a pleasant hilltop town with cobbled streets and a visible Indian presence. In the market some of the older women can be seen wearing traditional, brightly striped skirts. The town is noted for its basket-weaving and furniture workshops, which produce not just baskets but also sophisticated ornamental objects and high-quality wood and rattan furniture (see Shopping p 117). Nahuizalco is six kilometres north of (and uphill from) Sonsonate just off the highway to Apaneca and Ahuachapán. It is served by local buses and by Route 249, which continues to Ahuachapán.

Salcoatitán ★

A short distance further north is Salcoatitán, a simple town whose austere, 17th-century church has an interesting wooden interior. Nearby there remains in operation a very old and traditional *beneficio*, or coffee processing plant (visits by appointment only).

Juayúa ★

Right next door to Salcoatitán is, a more modern town whose big whitewashed church has twin steeples, plenty of stained glass, and a revered statue of a black Christ.

Apaneca ★★

The town of Apaneca lies further along in a very picturesque setting, with coffee plantations spreading through a series of valleys below and volcanoes visible in the distance above. This seems to be the only town in the region that has awakened to the possibilities of tourism. It boasts a very pleasant hotel, two interesting restaurants, and a couple of handicrafts shops. Its 17th-century church has a simple wooden interior. The mountain climate is agreeable, and the town receives a considerable flow of weekend visitors.

Eight kilometres northeast of Apaneca lies **Laguna Verde** ★, a mountain lake whose steep banks are covered in luxuriant tropical vegetation. It can be reached by a very rough road (four-wheel drive in the rainy season) or in 1½ hours by foot. The lake is very pretty to look at, but swimming is not advised because of the profusion of algae. For hiking see p 111.

Ahuachapán lies 14 km (9 mi) northwest of Apaneca, bringing us to the end of this route.

■ Ahuachapán

For travellers arriving from Guatemala, Ahuachapán (pronounced a-wa-cha-PAN) may be the first sizable town (population 90,000) they come upon in El Salvador. It lies 23 km (14 mi) from the border at Las Chinamas, and is rather a boring place. Don't despair — things get more interesting deeper inside the country.

There's no special reason to dawdle in Ahuachapán, but if you do, **Los Ausoles** ★ are worth a visit. These are a series of volcanic vents that set mud puddles boiling and sulphurous steam rising from crevices in a barren field, four kilometres southeast of the city along a rough dirt road *(occasional minibuses pass nearby; alternately, a pickup truck will take you there and back from the public market for about $5)*. Part of the area is fenced off and occupied by a geothermal electricity plant, kept under military guard. The rest forms an eery, stone-strewn landscape. Watch where you step—the ground may be hot. And shifts in wind direction can send hot, smelly steam your way.

Laguna El Espino, four kilometres west (2½ mi) of Ahuachapán and reached by any of three short dirt tracks from the highway, is a pleasant lake set in a breezy spot and suitable for bathing. At the eastern end of the lake is a small recreation area, open to the public.

■ Chalchuapa and the Ruins of El Tazumal ★

The town of Chalchuapa lies 21 km (13 mi) east of Ahuachapán and 13 km (8 mi) west of Santa Ana (Bus 236). It has several picturesque colonial streets, but the main point of interest is the ruins of **El Tazumal** ★ *(free admission; Tue to Sun, 9 a.m. to 7 p.m.)*, situated in the town itself just five minutes' walk from the highway along a clearly marked street (bus conductors will know where to let you off). The ruins are clearly visible even from a distance. There are snack bars and gift shops near the entrance.

El Tazumal was built in stages between the fifth and ninth centuries A.D. by Pipil Indians, who were related to the Aztecs of central Mexico and heavily influenced by Mayans living in what is now Guatemala and Honduras. Many centuries after they were abandoned, a large pyramid and several smaller structures were excavated in the late 1930s. After studying them, archeologists decided the best way to protect them against the elements was to entomb them in concrete, and the results of this tragic mistake remain evident today. The highest structure in the group is 23 m (75 ft) tall, although it looks taller. Unfortunately, everything is covered in ugly grey concrete, with the original stone exposed in only a few small spots. This renders the site much less impressive than it might be.

The site includes a small museum displaying a number of ceramic objects as well as some metal objects which are cited as evidence of trade with neighbouring societies. The archeological zone covers a much broader area than what has been excavated, much of it now lying beneath the town of Chalchuapa. At least one very high structure has been found further out, but excavation and restoration have been postponed for lack of funds.

■ **Lago de Güija** ★★

Lago de Güija (pronounced GWEE-ya) has not been developed for tourism. It has no restaurants or hotels, and it is hidden away on a back road. To get there, take the Santa Ana-Metapán highway. A short way before Metapán, near the signpost marking Kilometro 97 (the distance is measured from San Salvador), look for an unmarked dirt road on the left (on the right if you are heading south). By bus, take Route 235 and ask if the conductor knows where to let you off. After 2½ km (1½ mi) of rough road, just past an old railway bridge, there is a clearing, and then the lake. Fishermen can take you by boat from there along the 11-km (7 mi) length of the lake. The price is negotiable.

This long, shallow lake extending into Guatemala retains an enjoyably calm, off-the-beaten-track sort of pace. Ringed by low hills and by the San Diego volcano, it has an idyllic aspect and a timeless feel to it. Fishermen inhabit its shores, living from their catches of lake bass and crabs. Large stones with mysterious ancient carvings have been found on an island in the lake. Some of these stones are on display outside the building that housed the Museo Nacional in San Salvador.

■ **Metapán** ★

The sprawling market in this pleasant, hilly town has a rough-hewn aspect that sits in odd contrast with some of the town's genteel, cobbled streets with their red-tile-roofed houses and the ornate early 18th-century **Iglesia La Parroquia** with its splendid façade and its fine silver work near the main altar.

The road up from Santa Ana, 45 km (28 mi) to the south (Bus 235), has enjoyable, hilly scenery through sparsely populated countryside.

Metapán (pronounced may-ta-PAN) is the main jumping-off point for visits to the Montecristo nature reserve and cloud forest nearby.

Reserva Natural de Montecristo ★★

Montecristo, remote and hard to reach, contains El Salvador's only cloud forest and is devoted more to the preservation of rare plant and animal species than to visits by humans. Located in the mountains northeast of Metapán, this nature reserve and national park includes the spot where the borders of El Salvador, Guatemala and Honduras converge. For details, please see p 109.

Casco de la Hacienda see p 110.

Parks and Beaches

Parks

Parque Nacional de Cerro Verde ★★★ *($0.60 per vehicle plus $0.60 per person)* covers the slopes of Cerro Verde volcano and provides excellent views of the neighbouring Izalco and Santa Ana volcanoes. The Santa Ana volcano is the highest in El Salvador, soaring to 2,365 m (7,759 ft) above sea level. The road through the park climbs steadily for most of its 14-km (9 mi) length. To the right on the way up are dramatic aerial views of Lago de Coatepeque. With the change in altitude the air becomes cooler and the vegetation changes, with more coniferous trees.

Only at the top does it become clear that this is officially a national park. It is here that a park employee collects the entrance fee. There is an added charge of $0.60 to enter the grounds of the Hotel de Montaña, with its observation deck overlooking the Izalco volcano. For those travelling by bus, Route 248 operates several times daily from Santa Ana via El Congo. Schedules vary, so it is best to check with park staff to find out when the last one leaves (usually late afternoon). The park is accessible day and night.

Camping is possible, but visitors must obtain permission from the park superintendent, and this is not always a sure bet.

The simplest, shortest visit after arriving at Cerro Verde involves taking the three-minute hike from the parking area to the Hotel de Montaña, stepping onto the observation deck there, and snapping a few photographs of the Izalco volcano.

This volcano erupted with such ferocity in the late 18th century that its fires could be seen at night over great distances, visible even to sailors on the Pacific Ocean. Its most recent eruption was in 1957, and its cone now reaches a height of 1,910 m (6,266 ft) above sea level. The slopes remain devoid of vegetation, contributing to its dramatic appearance, and its black sides and almost perfect conical shape make it look just as you might expect a volcano to look. Morning visits provide a better chance of seeing the volcano unobstructed by cloud cover.

For hikes in the area, see p 111. One very short and easy hike involves on a 30-minute circuit from the Cerro Verde parking area on a trail that provides good views of the Santa Ana volcano and of Lago de Coatepeque.

Reserva Natural de Montecristo ★★ is a nature reserve with the status of a national park. It is hard to reach and little visited, which is probably just as well. It is an important breeding ground for endangered species, notably for the quetzal, that almost mythical bird with the long tail and brilliant plumage that earned an important place in the Central American spirit but was hunted almost to extinction. (The Guatemalan currency is named after it.) If hordes of so-called ecotourists were allowed to come trampling through during breeding season, they could well hasten the demise of this magnificent creature, which requires absolute silence when reproducing. Some areas of the park are off limits to visitors for much of the year for this reason. Permit requirements and poor road conditions are other deterrents to visitors. During rainy periods the road may be almost impassable.

Getting into the park takes about two hours from the town of Metapán along a very rough dirt road unsuited to ordinary automobiles. A short visit can be conducted in about three hours plus two hours to get back to Metapán. It is possible to do the trip in a single day from San Salvador, but this involves many hours on the road.

Among Montecristo's many distinctions are El Salvador's only remaining area of cloud forest and the spot where the borders of El Salvador, Guatemala and Honduras meet. Though the reserve includes territory from all three countries and part of it is jointly managed, it is accessible only from the Salvadoran side.

The cloud forest remains cool and damp year-round, producing very lush vegetation, including many species of orchids, which flower between late February and late April. Several species of trees growing here have disappeared elsewhere in the country. The highest area is called **El Trifinio**. At the pinnacle, up a steep path, are an obelisk and observation point marking the spot where the three countries meet. You can peer into all three at once if the cloud cover is not too thick.

Partway inside the park is an old village called **Casco de la Hacienda**, inhabited by about 200 families. The village fell into decay and is now being restored with financial help from the European Union. Simple rooms for overnight stays are available in small cabins there with permission from the *Departamento de Recursos Renovables y Vida Silvestre* (the address is given two paragraphs below).

Higher up, at an altitude of about 1,700 m (5,577 ft), are **Los Planes de Montecristo**, with an orchid garden and a small campsite. Vehicles cannot go much further. The final three kilometres to the pinnacle require a difficult one-hour hike in each direction, with the last kilometre rising steeply to an altitude of about 2,400 m (7,874 ft).

Before going, you should have a permit from the *Departamento de Recursos Renovables y Vida Silvestre* (Department of Renewable Resources and Forest Life) of the *Ministerio de Agricultura y Ganadería* (Ministry of Agriculture and Livestock), located in Colonia Santa Lucía in Ilopango, in the eastern suburbs of San Salvador. If you plan to stay overnight, this should be specified in the permit. Some accounts suggest it isn't always necessary to have a permit, but it is certainly better not to press your luck.

You should also have a very sturdy vehicle, preferably with four-wheel drive, especially during the rainy season. You can go on your own or in a group. Among those offering tours is Ricardo Cerna *(Librería Pitufina, Calle 15 de Septiembre, Metapán,* ☎ *442-0237)*. For a group leaving from Metapán, spending three hours in the reserve and returning to Metapán, the flat rate is $52 per group, with a pickup truck providing transport for up to 15 passengers. Those interested in an excursion can also inquire at the

Hotel San José in Metapán
(☎ 442-0556).

Sihuatehuacán, in Santa Ana, and **Atecozol**, in Izalco, near Sonsonate (both $0.60 per person plus $0.60 per vehicle; open every day 8 a.m. to 6 p.m.) are *turicentros*, established by the *Instituto Salvadoreño de Turismo* to make swimming pools, wooded parklands and picnic areas accessible to local families.

■ Beaches

The area around **Barra de Santiago** ★, about midway between Acajutla and the Guatemalan border at La Hachadura and several kilometres south of the main highway (served by infrequent buses from Ahuachapán), has some of the better beaches in western El Salvador. The sand is grey, but not as dark as in some other places. A long ribbon of sand is separated from the rest of the mainland by a mangrove-lined estuary. Simple eating places and very primitive lodgings are available for the more adventurous traveller. *(Hotel Las Cabañas in Apaneca, see p 114, can organize day trips to Barra de Santiago for guests, including a boat ride along the estuary.)*

Two small beach areas are situated nearer Acajutla, **Playa de Metalío** to the west and **Playa Los Cóbanos** to the east (both served by infrequent buses from Sonsonate). These attract day trippers from nearby towns, especially on weekends, but facilities are rather primitive and the beaches are not especially attractive. The latter has a dangerous undertow. Both have dark volcanic sand.

Outdoor Activities

Hiking

Parque Nacional de Cerro Verde ★★★ offers several good hiking possibilities. All trails run from the parking area near the summit. The shortest and easiest is a half-hour loop that provides good views of the Santa Ana volcano and Lago de Coatepeque. If you are more ambitious, there are trails going to the craters of both the Santa Ana and Izalco volcanoes. Santa Ana is a longer climb but easier because it is covered with vegetation and the footing is good. Izalco is lava-covered and slippery. In each case the climb to the top should take about two hours and the walk around the crater about one hour. The Santa Ana volcano has several concentric craters, one of them spewing clouds of sulphurous steam.

Laguna Verde ★, a mountain lake surrounded by luxuriant vegetation, is an easy 8-km walk from Apaneca, about 1½ hours in each direction.

In the **Reserva Natural de Montecristo** ★★★, hiking is the only way to reach El Trifinio, the uppermost portion of the reserve. At certain times of year it is off limits to visitors. Before setting off anywhere in the reserve, visitors should check with staff to see where hiking is permitted (see also p 109).

Swimming and Boating

Lago de Coatepeque and **Lago de Güija** are both suitable for swimming. At Lago de Coatepeque the easiest access is from the decks of the hotels. There may be a small fee. Most boating there is done by the owners of private estates that border the lake. At Lago de Güija, access for swimmers is simpler. Fishermen provide boat tours of the lake.

There is a strong undertow at most beaches along the Pacific coast, and swimmers should be especially cautious. At **Barra de Santiago**, swimmers can enjoy the calm waters of the estuary.

Bicycling

Terrain in much of western El Salvador is hilly, but inclines are rarely very steep. The road to Cerro Verde can be something of a challenge, however. The 36-km (22 mi) highway between Sonsonate and Ahuachapán is well paved and carries only light traffic. Although parts of it are hilly, the scenery is pleasing. Several moderately sized towns lie at short intervals along the way. The 40-km (25 mi) highway between Sonsonate and Santa Ana is also lightly travelled and very scenic, with many coffee plantations, but there are scarcely any towns along the way, which means there may be less security. The same applies to the otherwise pleasing 45-km (28 mi) highway between Santa Ana and Metapán.

Accommodation

■ Santa Ana

The best hotel by far in Santa Ana is the **Hotel Sahara** *($26, VI - MC; ≡, tv, ℜ; 10ª Avenida Sur, corner of 3ª Calle Poniente, ☎ 447-8865)*. Before the Sahara opened in 1992, Santa Ana was something of a desert in terms of comfortable lodgings. The hotel is situated at the edge of the city centre. Its 30 rooms, set around a small atrium, are bright and comfortably furnished. Most have balconies. Staff are friendly, and there is a secure parking area. The surrounding streets are not safe at night; taxis are suggested.

Hotel Libertad *($12; ⊕; 4ª Calle Oriente, corner of 1ª Avenida Norte, ☎ 441-2358)*, housed in an old two-story building one block north of the cathedral. It has a certain colonial charm, but its 11 rooms are dark and rather basic. Plumbing and lighting fixtures can cause problems. There are interesting views of the cathedral from the upstairs terrace.

Hotel International *($14; 25ª Calle Poniente near 10ª Avenida Sur, ☎ 440-0810 or 440-0804)*, is situated a short distance from the city centre. Its 15 brightly decorated rooms vary in size; some are quite tiny. Try for an inside room to avoid street noise. Furnishings in the common areas are rather eccentric.

Several cheaper and generally scruffier hotels, among them the **Hotel Livingston** *(☎ 441-1801)* and the **Pensión Monterrey** *(☎ 441-2738)* may be found near the corner of 8ª Avenida Sur and 9ª Calle Poniente.

■ Lago de Coatepeque

Hotel del Lago *($40-$46 new section, $23-$29 old section, VI - MC - AE; ☎ 446-9511)* has been around more than half a century. It sits on the north side of the lake, a bit further along the road than most of the other spots, and is well enough known that Lago de

Accommodation

Coatepeque suffices as an address. This 16-room hotel has plenty of character. From its open-air restaurant there are magnificent views of the lake. Rooms in the old section are enormous though somewhat bare, with high ceilings and dark red floor tiles. The newer rooms are smaller and more appealingly furnished.

Hotel Torremolinos *($23, VI - MC - AE - DC; ☎ 446-9437, ⇄ 441-1859)* seems almost a newer, simpler version of the Hotel del Lago just down the road. Its 15 rooms are clean and bright, and its restaurant also offers good lake views.

Amacuilco Guest House *($15; 200 m from the Antel office, ☎ 441-0608)* has an artsy, bohemian feel, rather uncommon in El Salvador. Posters for art and language classes catch the eye, and there is a weird and wonderful assortment of art pieces and knickknacks. The six rooms here are small and rather basic, with shared bath. Some of them are set on stilts over the lake, as are a small dining area and one of several lounges. The hotel can arrange tours to out-of-the-way spots in the area.

Balneario Obrero *(Lago de Coatepeque, near Ochupse Arriba; free with written permission from the Departamento de Bienestar Social of the Ministerio del Trabajo, Colonia San Bartolo, San Salvador)* was set up as a vacation spot for workers and their families by the aforementioned Social Welfare Department of the Ministry of Labour. Thirty-six simple cabins, each accommodating four people, are set on sprawling, landscaped grounds that include a big pool, a stretch of lake front, a meeting hall, and a communal kitchen. This government-run establishment is heavily used for weekend vacations and is sometimes provided to groups for midweek meetings. You don't have to be Salvadoran to apply for a free permit, although travellers should remember that local taxpayers end up footing the bill.

■ Cerro Verde

One of the most striking views of a volcano to be found anywhere on earth stares you right in the face at the **Hotel de Montaña** *($29 weekdays, no meals included; $46 to $58 Friday to Sunday, with one meal, VI - MC - AE - DC; ℜ, bar, gift shop; Cerro Verde national park, ☎ 271-2434 in San Salvador for reservations)*. From the broad observation terrace (and also from some of the rooms), you get an eagle's eye view of the Izalco volcano across the valley in all its stark glory. This modern, government-run hotel has something of an institutional atmosphere, and is busy during the day with tourists coming to see the volcano. It offers 20 big, comfortable rooms with fireplaces and with wooden floors and ceilings, a little like some of the lodges at national parks in the U.S. Weekend prices vary according to whether there is a volcano view from the room and whether breakfast or supper is chosen. The volcano last erupted shortly before the hotel was completed.

Camping is also possible in the park.

■ Sonsonate

The choice of hotels in this city of 90,000 people is truly dismal. Perhaps the least awful is the new **Hotel El Cairo** *($6, ⊕, corner of 4ª Avenida Sur and 2ª Calle Oriente)* with four rooms and six more under construction. The hotel is on a quiet side street near the city centre; rooms are small, bright and simple.

The unappealing, run-down **Hotel Orbe** (corner of 4ª Calle Oriente and 2ª Avenida Sur, ☎ 451-1416) is the biggest hotel in town, with 24 rooms set around a parking area; dim-witted staff could not even quote room rates!

Hotel Florida ($5; on 18ª Avenida Sur near the bus terminal, ☎ 451-0967) has 13 small, dark, dingy rooms with shared bath, but at least it is quiet. Nearby hotels are even worse.

Auto-Hotel Los Altos ($9; ℜ; on a dirt road just off the highway to Nahuizalco, two kilometres north of town, ☎ 451-2603) rents rooms more by the hour than by the night. Furnishings look like sets from a bad porno film, and each of the 12 rooms has enclosed parking to deter snoopers, but in a pinch it may have to do.

■ Acajutla

Lodgings here are scarcely better than in Sonsonate.

Motel El Greco ($10; ⊕, ℜ; 10 Calle, ☎ 452-3346) is a simple, family-run place with 12 rooms on a quiet street a few minutes' walk from the centre of town.

Motel Miramar ($7; ⊕, ≈, ℜ; Calle Barrios Peña facing the sea, ☎ 452-3183), has four basic, dilapidated rooms, which seem to be a neglected appendage to an appealing seafront restaurant.

Hotel Santimone ($15; ⊕; next to Restaurant Kilo 2, on the highway two kilometres north of town) has 21 very ordinary rooms on a site in the middle of nowhere.

■ Juayúa

Hotel y Restaurante Típico ($10, corner of 1 Calle Poniente and Merceditas Cáceres, no phone) has small, simple rooms facing a small garden. Downstairs rooms have private bath and upstairs rooms do not, but there is no difference in price.

■ Apaneca

Hotel y Restaurante Las Cabañas ($40, VI - MC; ☎ 279-0099 in San Salvador for reservations) is quite simply the most appealing place to stay in western El Salvador. Perched on a high plateau at the edge of town, this recently opened mountain inn has gorgeous views of lush valleys planted in coffee. A group of seven cabins are set amid pretty gardens. Interiors are decorated simply but tastefully, with colourful bedspreads and wall decorations. Three of the cabins have additional bedrooms and can accommodate between four and eight people ($46 to $58). One has a fireplace. The climate is fresh and pleasant. The hotel can arrange excursions to a coffee plantation, processing plant and private orchid garden, to Laguna Verde, and to Barra de Santiago beach. Friendly staff.

■ Ahuachapán

Hotel Casa Blanca Boarding House ($17-$21; some rooms ≡, light meals; corner of Calle Barrios and 2 Avenida Norte, ☎ 443-1505, ↹ 443-1503) may be your best bet in town. Located on a quiet corner three blocks from the market, this low colonial-style building has a small courtyard and a pleasant lobby and sitting area. Friendly and family-run, the hotel has eight rooms that are large and pleasant although rather simple. Snacks and light meals are available.

Hotel y Restaurant Gran Rancho *($11 ⊕; on the highway just west of town, ☎ 443-1820)* is just down the hill at the western edge of town. Its 10 rooms are clean but very small and simple.

Hotel El Parador, two kilometres west of town, looked more promising but was still under construction when we visited.

Hotel San José *($10, $11 ⊗; 6 Calle Poniente in front of Parque Menéndez, ☎ 443-1820)*, located in the middle of town; its 12 rooms are hot, dark and poorly furnished.

■ **Chalchuapa**

Hotel y Restaurant El Cordobés *($14 pb, $9 shared; ⊕; 13 Avenida Norte by the main highway, ☎ 444-0532)* is a small new hotel, with six simply furnished rooms, situated near the ruins of El Tazumal.

■ **Metapán**

Hotel San José *($18; ≡, tv, ℜ; along the highway next to the market, ☎ 442-0556)* is really the only show in town. The 27 rooms in this modern four-story building are decently furnished and have balconies, some with good mountain views, but there is no elevator.

Restaurants

Dining is western El Salvador is always casual, and reservations are virtually never required. Supper hour is somewhat earlier than in the capital. Menus tend to stick faithfully to a limited variety of tried-and-true dishes. It is difficult to point to any regional specialties. Vegetarians are poorly catered for, except at breakfast. The usual fried chicken joints abound in the larger towns; pizza and hamburgers are usually easy to find. And, of course, even in the village markets there are always *pupusas*, those cheese- or bean-stuffed tortillas—one reliable solution for vegetarians. Here is a brief glance at some of the better restaurants in the region.

■ **Santa Ana**

La Canoa *(main courses $5 to $10; 3 Avenida Sur near 5 Calle Poniente)* offers many steak and seafood items, with some original dishes such as baked shrimp wrapped in squid. Tables are set around an open terrace. Seats are somewhat uncomfortable.

Los Horcones *(inexpensive; next to the cathedral)* specializes in tacos and burgers. This is a pleasant, open-air restaurant spread over two levels, with wooden furniture and plenty of greenery.

El Tucán *(main courses $4 to $10; Avenida Independencia between 9 and 11 Calles Oriente)* specializes in steaks. It has a pleasant upstairs terrace.

Kiyomi *(main courses $3 to $5; 4 Avenida Sur between 3 and 5 Calles Poniente)* offers a variety of fish, steak and chicken dishes as well as chow mein and sandwiches. The dining room is quite ordinary apart from a few Japanese drawings.

■ **Lago de Coatepeque and Cerro Verde**

Hotel restaurants are your best bet here.

The restaurant of the **Hotel del Lago** (see p 112; main courses $6 to $10) is renowned for its views of the lake and for its crab soup. Main courses include *guapote*, a somewhat muddy-tasting lake bass, and a variety of meat and shrimp dishes. Service is sometimes slow.

The restaurant of **Hotel Torremolinos** (see p 113; main courses $5 to $8) also has splendid views of the lake and a good variety of seafood dishes.

At the **Hotel de Montaña** in Parque Nacional de Cerro Verde (see p 113), the restaurant and bar face the Izalco volcano. On weekdays the heavily meat-oriented menu offers main courses for $4 to $7; on weekends there is a buffet for $9.

■ **Sonsonate and Acajutla**

The lack of choice means travellers will have to go native here. There are many small restaurants and *comedores* in Sonsonate, but nothing really to shout about. In Acajutla, several open-air restaurants along the seashore offer a variety of fish and seafood dishes.

Restaurant Acajutla (main courses $3 to $8), on the eastern edge of town, is the biggest, noisiest and most popular. It has an extensive menu and sometimes offers live music.

Restaurant Miramar, on the main street in the centre of town, is an open-air restaurant with a pleasant seaside setting.

■ **Juayúa**

Despite its name, **Rincón Suizo** has little that's Swiss apart from some travel posters. Open only from Friday to Sunday, it has tables both indoors and outdoors facing the central plaza and the church. The house specialty is baked leg of pork with gravy ($4.50). Most meat and seafood dishes are $5 to $7.

Oskar's, behind the church, is a bright, simple place whose menu includes meat dishes and sandwiches.

■ **Apaneca**

The restaurant of **Hotel Las Cabañas** (main courses $4 to $8) is open daily and offers magnificent views of coffee-growing country. This is an open-air restaurant with a lofty wood roof. Specialties include crab soup and a selection of veal dishes (see p 114).

La Casita de Mi Abuela, in the centre of town, is open Saturday and Sunday only. It is decorated with a profusion of painted tiles and stained glass, and it also has an extravagant garden terrace.

■ **Ahuachapán**

There isn't much in the centre of town, but along the highway about two kilometres west of town there is a trio of restaurants — **El Parador**, **El Paseo** and **La Posada** — that are cheerful and inexpensive. Menus emphasize steak.

Entertainment

We're not talking big-time night life here. Even in Santa Ana, the biggest city in western El Salvador, the sidewalks tend to get rolled up pretty early. This is partly because of conservative tradition and partly for fear of crime. Most street activity peters out by about 7 p.m. and not much later on weekends. Cinemas often draw their biggest crowds for late afternoon showings. Evening presentations have occasionally been cancelled when nobody shows up. Your best bet, in Santa Ana as elsewhere in the region, is to have a leisurely dinner and then curl up with a good book.

■ **Santa Ana**

Plays and performances are occasionally put on at the **Teatro Nacional de Santa Ana** close to the Parque Central. This option may prove worth exploring.

Shopping

Generally, the choice of distinctive items is rather slim. Some shops sell handicrafts from other parts of the country and from Guatemala, but prices and variety fail to match what can be found in San Salvador.

Practical, day-to-day necessities can usually be found at small shops or public markets in the larger towns, or at the **Siman** department store in Santa Ana.

■ **Nahuizalco**

The small town of Nahuizalco, just north of Sonsonate, offers some of the most interesting shopping in western El Salvador. The town is noted for its skilled basket weavers, who produce much more than baskets. These artisans weave some very elaborate ornamental objects in a variety of shapes, some of them resembling animals. As well, there is at least one workshop in town that produces attractive wooden and wicker furniture. These items are sold at several shops along the main street between the entrance to town and the market. Do not forget that it is up to travellers to get these sometimes bulky objects back home. Vendors generally do not take care of shipping. Tourists are still regarded as something of a novelty here, and most production goes out through middlemen, who tack on big margins. Shoppers may also find some locally produced pottery and cloth.

■ **Sonsonate, Ahuachapán and Chalchuapa**

In Sonsonate and Ahuachapán, belts and a small variety of other leather items can be found at stalls in the public markets. In Chalchuapa, near the entrance to the ruins of El Tazumal, several shops sell reproductions of ancient pottery and ceramic objects. They also offer good selections of masks.

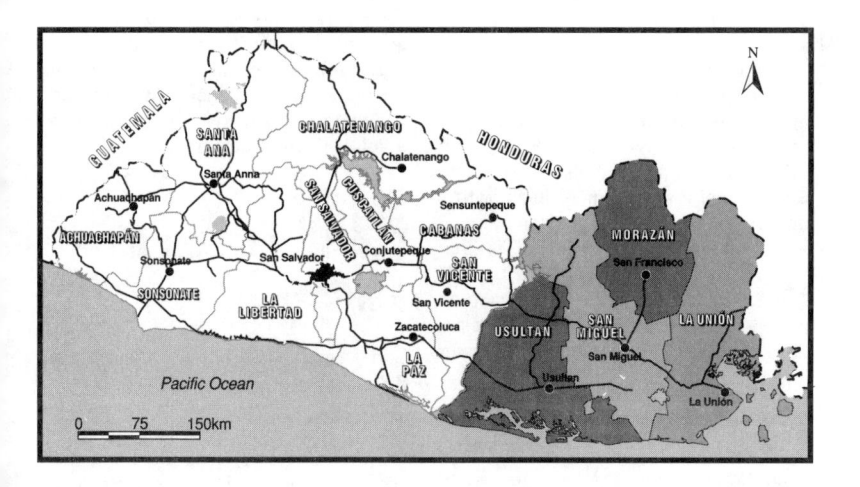

EASTERN EL SALVADOR

The eastern part of El Salvador still bears scars from the combat that ravaged the country during its twelve-year civil war that ended early in 1992. The heaviest and most persistent fighting between guerrilla and government forces, with the greatest loss of life, occurred in the eastern part of the country. The 1992 peace agreement lifted a huge yoke from the shoulders of eastern El Salvador, and people can now get on with their lives.

One place where memories of the war are preserved is the new *Museo de la Revolución Salvadoreña* (Museum of the Salvadoran Revolution), established in the northern hillside town of **Perquín**. For much of the war Perquín was the rebels' unofficial capital. The zone to its south was utterly devastated, but today it is clear that resettling is under way, a sign that people are looking to the future with greater hope.

Other parts of the region offer a panoply of attractions. The hilly country west of San Miguel has many stretches of road with gorgeous views of valleys below and volcanoes above. Picturesque towns and villages provide a special blend of old-fashioned charm and mountain vistas. East of San Miguel lies the colourful market town of **Santa Rosa de Lima**. To the south and southeast are several small beach resorts, some with pleasant places to stay. The port city of **La Unión** holds little interest. It does, however, lie near the attractive hillside town of **Conchagua** and is the jumping-off point for islands in the **Gulf of Fonseca**, from

Eastern El Salvador

which both Honduras and Nicaragua are visible in the distance.

The valley of the Río Lempa forms a natural boundary between the central and eastern parts of El Salvador. The four administrative departments comprising the eastern region are Usulután, San Miguel and La Unión, each with a departmental capital of the same name, and Morazán, whose capital is San Francisco Gotera. The town of **El Amatillo**, lying along the Río Goascorán in La Unión department, is the principal border crossing between El Salvador and southern Honduras.

As in other regions of El Salvador, the topography in the east is marked by a solid ridge of mountainous terrain to the north and a broad coastal plain in the south, punctuated by a series of upland ridges and volcanic peaks, the most imposing of which is **Chaparrastique**, also known as the **San Miguel volcano**. The centre of the region is characterized by rugged hills and fertile valleys.

San Miguel is by far the biggest town in the eastern region, with the best hotels and the most restaurants. Unlike Santa Ana in the west, San Miguel is quite far from San Salvador and does not fall under its direct shadow. Hence many people choose to conduct business here rather than in the capital, which means San Miguel is a busy city. It is also a natural base for visiting other parts of the region. Elsewhere lodgings tend to be more rudimentary, although comfortable hotels can be found along a couple of the beaches.

A visit to eastern El Salvador should include a day exploring the countryside and some of the small towns west of San Miguel. (This is feasible by bus, though much more time-consuming.) Part of another day should be set aside for Perquín, a rugged mountain town and home to the museum of the revolution, with a side trip to Santa Rosa de Lima on the way back. Consider also including a day or two of relaxation by a volcanic sand beach.

Finding Your Way Around

■ **By Car**

San Miguel, 136 km (84 mi) east of San Salvador, is by far the most important highway hub in the eastern part of the country. It lies along the Carretera Panamericana (Pan-American Highway), which traverses El Salvador from west to east and crosses the Honduran border at El Amatillo.

Parts of this important highway are in rough shape, with gaping potholes in a few places. A short distance east of San Salvador, it narrows to two lanes despite heavy volumes of traffic, and speeds tend to be slow. (Rumour has it that officials linked with the Christian Democratic Party, fraudulently deprived of power until the 1984 election, made up for lost time by lining their pockets quickly while in power, and that money allocated to improve this highway formed part of the booty. Whether or not this is true, it is widely believed.) Farther east there are a couple of good but short stretches of four-lane highway.

An important bridge called Puente Cuscatlán, which crossed the Río Lempa next to a big hydroelectric plant, fell victim to rebel sabotage in 1983, and since then traffic on the Carretera Panamericana has been carried on a pair of hastily assembled Bailey bridges. These temporary bridges remain in service.

A similar fate befell another bridge, the Puente de Oro, along the Carretera del Litoral (coastal highway) further south. Traffic on that highway now crosses the Río Lempa along a parallel railway bridge. The so-called coastal highway is really an inland highway that runs parallel to the coast and passes through the city of Usulután. This is a shorter route if you are travelling to Usulután from San Salvador or from the Costa del Sol. Further west, in La Libertad department, it is a true coastal highway running through hilly terrain.

From San Miguel, highways radiate west to San Salvador, southwest to Usulután, south to the coast at El Cuco, southeast to La Unión, east to Santa Rosa de Lima and El Amatillo, and north to San Francisco Gotera and Perquín. Speeds have to be limited voluntarily in many places because of an abundance of potholes, although some highways are in better shape than others. Travellers just have to play it by ear.

Secondary roads, less subject to battering by heavy trucks, are sometimes in better shape than main highways. Most secondary roads are paved, but a few of the dirt roads are difficult to negotiate in ordinary cars. During the war, traffic in the region was constrained by army roadblocks or by fear of attack. This is no longer the case. Most drivers, however, avoid travel after dark for fear of common criminals. There are also the usual hazards of wandering livestock and disabled vehicles parked alongside the road.

Car Rental

At last word, rental cars were still not available in eastern El Salvador. Car rental agencies operate only in San Salvador and at the international airport south of the capital.

■ By Bus

As part of their campaign of economic sabotage during the 1980s, guerrilla forces often attacked buses in eastern El Salvador, ordering the passengers off and then setting the vehicles ablaze. More than 1,000 buses were destroyed in this fashion. The bus fleet has now been replenished, and service has returned to or surpassed prewar levels. Buses here as elsewhere in the country are cheap, frequent, slow and cramped.

San Miguel

There are hourly express buses between San Miguel and San Salvador (with extra service at busy times and final departures in late afternoon), which do the 136-km (84 mi) trip in about 2½ hours. Seating is just as cramped as in ordinary buses, but they use newer vehicles and do not take standing passengers. The fare is the equivalent of $2.25, which is 50 % higher than in the regular, slower buses.

Each intercity bus route is numbered, with route numbers and destinations painted right onto the bus.

The bus terminal in San Miguel is located in the central part of the city on 6ª Calle Oriente between 8ª and 10ª Avenidas Norte. Information can sometimes be obtained by telephone, ☎ 661-3784.

Routes from San Miguel include:

- 301 to San Salvador
- 320 to Playa El Cuco
- 324 to La Unión
- 330 to Santa Rosa de Lima and El Amatillo
- 332-B to Perquín
- 333 to Chinameca
- 385 to Playa El Tamarindo and other eastern beaches.

La Unión

The bus terminal in La Unión is located in the central part of the city on 3ª Calle Poniente near 4ª Avenida Norte.

Routes from La Unión include:

- 304 to San Salvador
- 324 to San Miguel
- 342 to Santa Rosa de Lima
- 353 to El Amatillo and the Honduran border
- 382 to Conchagua
- 383 to Playa El Tamarindo and other eastern beaches.

Other Destinations

In Usulután the terminal is situated along the main highway near the eastern edge of town. In most of the smaller towns buses leave from areas near the central markets. They can also be flagged at many points along the highway. In El Amatillo, on the Honduran border, buses leave from the border post.

Other routes include:

- 302 San Salvador—Usulután
- 306 San Salvador—Santa Rosa de Lima.

Again, this list is far from comprehensive. Some routes operate more frequently than others. On busier routes there is service several times an hour. Reliable information on departure times is available only at the terminals.

■ By Taxi

Taxis may be hired at any of the larger towns for trips around the region. Be sure to advise the driver of your itinerary and how much time you expect to spend at each place, and agree on a price beforehand. For half-day excursions this is cheaper than renting a car, and even for full-day excursions it may cost only slightly more.

■ By Air

Yes, believe it or not, regular air service is operated within tiny El Salvador. During the war, this was a popular means of business travel between San Salvador and the eastern part of the country because of the unpredictable state of the roads. Even the Carretera Panamericana was sometimes closed because of fighting.

Now that road travel has returned to normal, the number of air passengers has tapered off, but Transportes Aéreos de El Salvador (TAES) operates up to three daily flights to eastern El Salvador from the old Aeropuerto de Ilopango, which lies just off the Carretera Panamericana near the eastern outskirts of San Salvador. Before 1980, this was the main international airport. Since then it has served mostly as a military airport.

The TAES flights go to San Miguel and sometimes continue to San Francisco Gotera, Santa Rosa de Lima or La Unión, according to demand. There are small airstrips on fields outside each of these towns. Taxis can be phoned for pickups at the San Miguel airstrip.

Elsewhere, passengers should arrange in advance to be met.

The low-flying light aircraft used on these flights offer good aerial views of Lago de Ilopango and several volcanoes. Fares are reasonable (e.g., $26 one way from San Salvador to San Miguel), but flights operate only if there is a minimum number of passengers; it is essential to check ahead.

For information
TAES
Aeropuerto de Ilopango
☎ 295-0280, 295-0363, 295-0312 and 295-0349.

★ Exploring

■ San Miguel ★

Lying in the shadow of Chaparrastique volcano, San Miguel is the third largest city in El Salvador, with a population of 220,000. Only San Salvador and Santa Ana are bigger. Some *Migueleños* (as inhabitants of San Miguel call themselves) assert that their city is bigger than Santa Ana. Regardless of what the statistics say, San Miguel certainly feels bigger. Since the war ended, it has become something of a boom town as pent-up investment is released. Two big shopping centres have been built, based on forecasts that people in the surrounding area are going to have more money to spend. The economy of the region is diversified, with coffee, sugar cane, cattle and cotton all playing significant roles.

Most of the recent projects and all of the more comfortable hotels have been built toward the outskirts of the city.

The rather plain city centre bustles by day as traders spill over from the market into nearby streets, though it is quiet at night. This is an old city, founded in 1530 by the Spanish conquerors, but most of it was destroyed in a volcanic eruption in 1655. Many deliberate acts of demolition have taken place since then, and few historical buildings survive.

The 18th-century **Cathedral**, near the central plaza, is big and rather bare. Another old church, **Iglesia Medalla Milagrosa**, is prettier and is set in a park on 7ª Avenida Norte near 4ª Calle Poniente. Visiting a cemetery is not to everyone's taste, but the sprawling **Cementerio General** ★ along Avenida Roosevelt is worth seeing for its ornate and very elaborate mausoleums.

One kilometre north of San Miguel is the **Turicentro Altos de la Cueva**, providing swimming pools, dressing rooms, gardens, restaurants, and various sporting facilities (see p 130).

■ Chinameca ★★

The town of Chinameca lies 20 km (12 mi) west of San Miguel by the Carretera Panamericana and then four kilometres south from a cutoff. Bus 333 covers this route.

This is an attractive colonial town with hilly, cobbled streets and a picturesque church with fountains and statues in its garden. Although there is nothing of extraordinary interest here, it is an agreeable place for a stroll and is a striking example of what many Central American towns looked like a generation or two ago. The surrounding countryside is hilly and lush, with Chaparrastique volcano looming in the distance.

Just beyond the outskirts, one kilometre along a rough road skirting the cemetery, are **Los Ausoles de la Viejona** ★, which translates literally as spouts of the old lady. Here sulphurous steam rises from volcanic vents and puddles of mud are kept at a steady boil by geothermal energy. Some local people bring carefully wrapped food to cook in these puddles. They say it enhances the flavour.

■ **San Jorge**

San Jorge is reached by several roads running through this picturesque and hilly region. It is served by Bus 321-A from San Miguel and 371-A from Usulután. The area was off limits to most visitors during the war because of heavy fighting.

This is a fairly ordinary country town, but it is distinguished by the great beauty of the surrounding countryside and the scenic roads that lead to it. The road from San Miguel runs past the base of 2,130 metre-high (6,988 ft) Chaparrastique volcano, and as the road climbs there are dramatic views of plains and valleys in several directions. The road from Chinameca runs through coffee country and provides similarly breath-taking vistas. On the descent to El Tránsito, along the highway to Usulután, are distant glimpses of the Pacific Ocean.

■ **Berlín** ★

Berlín lies nine kilometres (5½ mi) south of Mercedes Umaña, the village lying at the junction with the Carretera Panamericana. Bus 354 provides this connection.

This is a poor mountain town, with visible reminders of the war. A number of buildings remain pockmarked by machine-gun fire. The rugged countryside is well suited to guerrilla warfare, and Berlín, seen as something of a rebel stronghold, was subjected to heavy attacks. This is one of the highest towns in El Salvador, and there is fine mountain scenery on the approaches, with panoramic views of distant valleys.

Four kilometres east of Berlín, along the treacherous dirt road leading to Santiago de María, lies the village of Alegría, which literally means happiness. Nearby is the **Laguna de Alegría** ★, a clear mountain lake fed by hot and cold springs and suitable for swimming. The road skirts the 1,600 metre-high (5,249 ft) Volcán de San Juan Tecapa.

■ **Ozatlán** ★

Ozatlán lies nine kilometres (5½ mi) northwest of Usulután, one kilometre off the highway (½ mi) to Santiago de María. Bus 488 runs from Usulután to Ozatlán; bus 349 runs more frequently, bypassing Ozotlán and continuing north to Santiago de María and El Triunfo at the junction with the Carretera Panamericana.

This is a small picture-postcard town with cobbled streets, red-tile roofs, a big central plaza, and a relaxed pace. As you leave Ozatlán heading northeast, you can catch stunning views of the Usulután volcano, known locally as Cerro Las Nieves, literally Snowy Hill, although snow is very rare.

■ **Usulután**

This is a hot, sprawling, scruffy market town and departmental capital lying on the coastal plain. There is little here to tempt visitors, but it does straddle the

Exploring 125

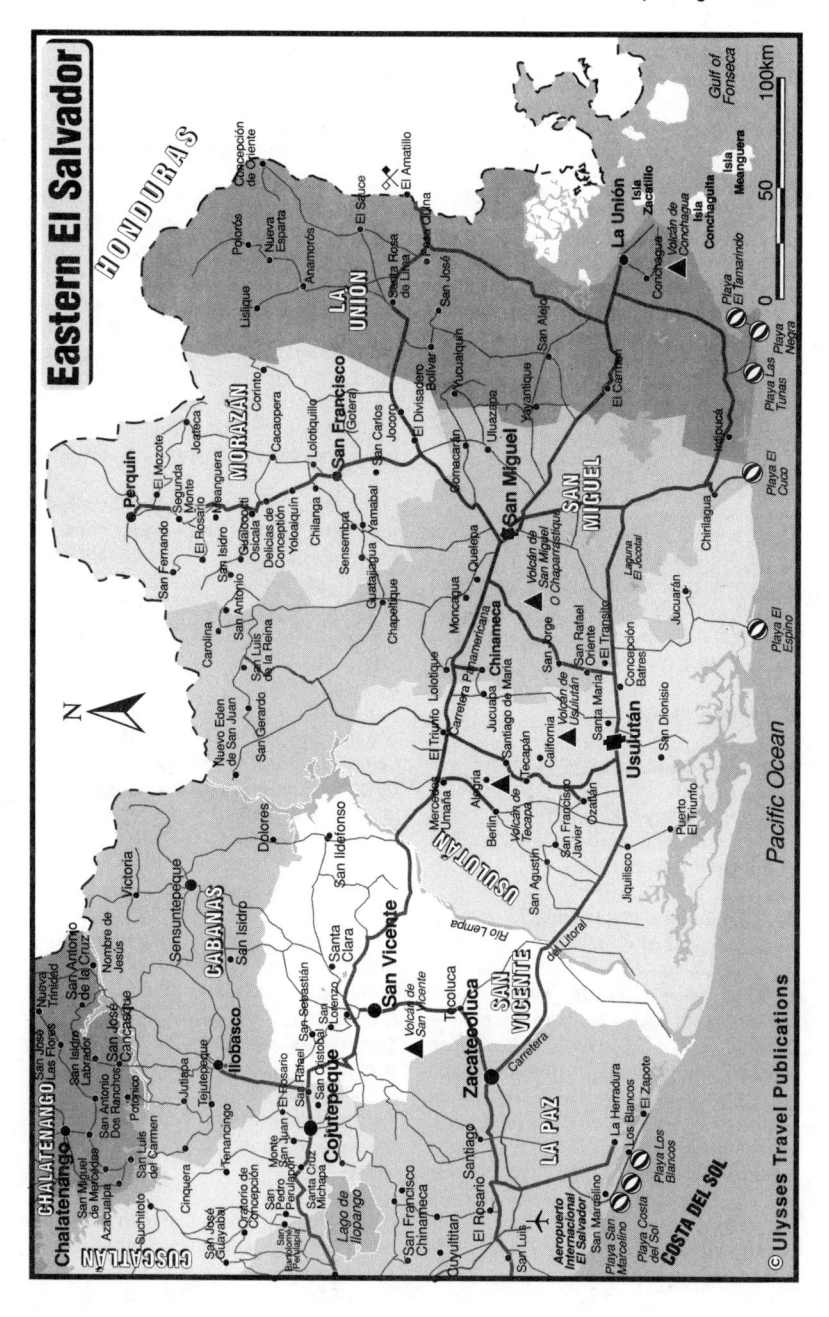

Eastern El Salvador

coastal highway and is an important transit point.

Laguna de Jocotal ★ is situated 23 km (14 mi) east of Usulután and offers good opportunities for bird watching (see p 129).

The best beach in the area, although it is not a very good one, is **Playa El Espino**, which lies 12 km (7½ mi) east along the Carretera del Litoral and then 22 km (13½ mi) south along a rough dirt road. It has only a few primitive eating spots and a dangerous undertow.

■ Playa El Cuco ★

This broad, smooth and very long beach of volcanic sand is a popular weekend spot with people from San Miguel, 39 km (24 mi) to the north with dramatic mountain scenery along the highway (see p 130).

■ Eastern Beaches ★★

A string of beaches extends from Playa El Tamarindo to Playa Las Tunas, covering many kilometres of the eastern coastline southwest of the Gulf of Fonseca (see p 130).

■ La Unión and the Islands of the Gulf of Fonseca

La Unión lies near the southeastern corner of El Salvador and faces the narrow Gulf of Fonseca, which also washes the shores of Honduras and Nicaragua. There are many fishermen, and the suburb of **Cutuco** is an important commercial seaport. The roads leading here cross flat, uninspiring terrain. The water at the small, scruffy beach in town is filthy. The town itself is hot, bustling and nondescript, with poor accommodations and little to tempt visitors unless they are headed to one of the islands in the Gulf of Fonseca.

Isla Meanguera

Small boats leave daily from the *embarcadero* (wharf) two blocks below the central plaza in La Unión bound for **Isla Meanguera** (pronounced may-an-GAY-ra) to the southeast. Normal departure time is 10:30 a.m., but it may be earlier or later, depending on tidal conditions. The trip takes a little under two hours (don't forget your sunhat), and the fare is $1.20 one way. The return trip leaves early each morning at 4 a.m.

Playa Majahual is the biggest beach on the island. Very simple accommodations are available in crude shelters with hammocks. You can also find beds or hammocks in private homes, as well as several small eating places and food shops. Fishing is the main source of livelihood for the small resident community on the island, which lies well off the beaten track. Isla Meanguera can also be visited as a day excursion by private arrangement with boatmen at the *embarcadero* in La Unión for a price of about $50.

Isla Zacatillo and Isla Conchaguita

Two smaller islands lying closer to the mainland, **Isla Zacatillo** and, midway between Zacatillo and Meanguera, **Isla Conchaguita**, are easily reachable for short visits. Isla Zacatillo has several secluded beaches, stony in places. A private boat trip costs about $40. Neither island offers lodgings or food. Be sure to bring your own refreshments.

Boatmen in La Unión can also take you to the Nicaraguan port of Potosí. There are immigration offices in both places, and the cost of the journey is about $120.

■ Conchagua ★

This is a breezy, hillside town about five kilometres (3 mi) south of La Unión (Bus 382) with good views of the surrounding countryside. Facing the central plaza, there is a pretty pale beige and blue church, built in 1693, with interesting carvings at the altar and religious statues in glass cases near the entrance. The 1,240 metre-high (4,068 ft) Conchagua volcano lies nearby. See page 131 for information on hiking up the volcano.

■ Santa Rosa de Lima ★

This bustling market town lies 40 km (25 mi) east of San Miguel and 18 km (11 mi) west of the Honduran border at El Amatillo. For travellers just arriving from Honduras or Nicaragua, this is a good introduction to El Salvador. The streets in the centre of town are crowded with market vendors. Facing the **central park**, which has now been taken over by market stalls, is a colonial church with a beautiful blue and white façade. There are many Hondurans among those who come to buy and sell. Items on offer include colourful hammocks and blankets.

Santa Rosa de Lima is also home to a restaurant, **La Pema**, famed for its seafood soup (see p 136). On the outskirts is a recreational area with swimming pools and other facilities, the **Complejo Turístico Limeño** (see p 130). Street names are not used much in the centre of the town. Addresses are usually given by referring to the nearest prominent building.

■ San Francisco Gotera

San Francisco Gotera, 31 km (19 mi) north of San Miguel (Bus 328), is capital of Morazán department, one of the most hilly, least fertile and least populated parts of El Salvador and also one of the poorest. It was in this department that FMLN rebels drew some of their most dedicated support in the civil war. As a result, it was the scene of fierce anti-insurgency activity by the army, and heavy fighting drove many inhabitants to seek refuge elsewhere. Despite years of peace, San Francisco Gotera remains a barracks town. It is one of the few places in the country that still has a very visible military presence not in response to any current threat but merely as a result of inertia.

This hilly town has little of particular interest. In a small hilltop park near the centre of town, there is a monument to General Francisco Morazán, the Honduran who strove valiantly but in vain to maintain Central American unity in the 1830s. This spot is worth seeing not so much for the monument itself but for the views over the town and the surrounding countryside.

■ Perquín ★★★

If Central American politics and history leave you totally indifferent, that may change after a visit to this town. Nobody can pass through here without being sensitized to important aspects of El Salvador's recent past. If revolutionary romanticism has ever entered your soul, or if you merely want to see how a ragged mountain town is faring in the post-civil-war period, you may find it interesting, even a little enlightening.

Perquín became a sort of unofficial capital for the *Frente Farabundo Martí de Liberación Nacional* (FMLN), the guerrilla movement that fought government forces for more than 12 years until a peace agreement was signed in 1992. Although the guerrillas were not dislodged from the town, they were subjected to heavy attacks, including aerial bombing raids, and a large part of the civilian populace fled. Most of those who remained were loyal FMLN supporters. Many others have now returned.

The town lies at the end of a pothole-riddled paved highway about 40 km (25 mi) north of San Francisco Gotera. The road winds through stark, mountainous countryside, and even the untrained eye can spot places that must have been ideal for ambushes. It is easy to see how guerrilla bands could have moved undetected through these hills. On flatter ground are small herds of cattle or fields under cultivation. A few houses remain abandoned, but in other places small makeshift dwellings have gone up recently. Little by little this zone is becoming repopulated after the devastation wrought by war.

The last few kilometres of road are badly deteriorated. Stretches of it have become totally unpaved, partly because of unrepaired damage from wartime bombing. Perquín lies near the top of a long hill, and more delicate vehicles should be parked by the entrance to the town. The streets are very roughly paved with large stones that become slippery when wet.

If you come by bus (Route 328-B from San Miguel or San Francisco Gotera), be sure to get an early start. The trip is slow (it can take nearly three hours from San Miguel), and the last bus back leaves in the early afternoon. If you miss it you can try to hitch a ride, or you can stay at the shabby Casa de Huéspedes El Gigante, on a side road below the cemetery near the entrance to the town, which charges $3 for dormitory beds.

Perquín has a rough-hewn but intimate feel to it. It was a poor mountain town before the war, and it remains so now. The **church**, facing the central plaza, has a bright mural on its façade depicting the slain archbishop Oscar Romero, a hero to many of the poor in El Salvador. The altitude is about 1,200 m (3,937 ft), and the climate is pleasant.

The highlight of most visits is the **Museo de la Revolución Salvadoreña ★★★** *($1.20, half price for Salvadorans; Tue to Sun, 9 a.m. to 4 p.m.)* is located about 300 m (984 ft) up the hill from the central plaza. This simple but compelling museum was opened by the FMLN at the end of 1992 and is housed in a cluster of small buildings, with outdoor displays also.

The visit begins with portraits and brief biographies of revolutionary heroes from El Salvador and other Latin American countries, moving next to photos depicting the dire poverty in El Salvador that motivated a revolutionary quest for social justice. Further along are photos depicting the hard daily lives of guerrilla fighters and exhibits of personal effects belonging to some who did not survive. Other parts of the museum display weaponry and radio equipment used by guerrillas as well as solidarity posters from many countries.

Outdoor displays include pieces of military helicopters shot down by rebel gunners. One of those helicopters carried Lt.-Col. Domingo Monterrosa to his death in 1984. The U.S.-trained Monterrosa had led the elite Atlacatl battalion of the Salvadoran army in the 1981 massacre of at least 500 civilians at the village of El Mozote in what probably ranks as the war's single most horrible action. El Mozote lies near Perquín, and the museum has a memorial for the victims. Just behind the museum is the crater left by a 230 kg (500 lbs) bomb. The crater is big enough to swallow a large house.

The museum also has a gift shop selling books and souvenirs. One item recently for sale was a coffee table with the barrels of M-16 automatic rifles as legs! There is a big open-air restaurant a few steps down the hill offering simple meals.

Some visitors may find the vision of history presented here to be one-sided, but there is no pretence of anything else. The museum was established by a revolutionary organization to tell things its own way, and this is done with remarkably little bitterness or rhetoric. In a spirit of enterprise, the museum brings visitors and economic activity to a lonely corner of the country and provides jobs for the former guerrilla fighters on staff. Its setting, in an area that witnessed the country's recent history with such intensity, creates a special immediacy, and its rustic ambiance, with livestock wandering freely through the grounds, maintains a closeness with the peasant roots of so many of the guerrilla fighters. The fact that a museum such as this can now exist in a country with a long tradition of political intolerance should be interpreted as a sign of hope.

■ **Segunda Monte**

Segunda Monte is a new town about midway between Perquín and San Francisco Gotera, settled by former guerrilla fighters trying to carve a civilian existence for themselves. The town has received European support in erecting clusters of simple new concrete dwellings, and a shoe factory and clothing factory are up and running. There's nothing really special to see, but the town provides another sign of the efforts being made by ex-guerrillas to build new lives and to resettle the area.

■ **El Mozote**

El Mozote, closer to Perquín, lies five kilometres from the highway along a dirt road so rough that it is nearly as fast to walk as to go by vehicle. El Mozote is a poor, bedraggled village that was the site of the notorious 1981 massacre and was virtually abandoned for a number of years. A simple memorial plaque pays homage to the victims.

Parks and Beaches

■ **Parks**

Laguna de Jocotal ★ offers good opportunities for bird watching and is officially a protected area, although few resources are devoted to protecting it. It is located along the Carretera del Litoral near the Km 132 marker 23 km (14 mi) east of Usulután and then three kilometres (2 mi) south along a lava-covered side road. This small, shallow lake abounds in bird life including a variety of herons, grebes and ducks. A few fishermen work here and will take visitors out in their canoes. There is also a trail around the lake just beyond its swampy shores. It is quiet and remote, with views of Chaparrastique volcano to the north and coastal hills to the south.

Eastern El Salvador

Altos de la Cueva *($0.60 per person plus $0.60 per vehicle; open every day 8 a.m. to 6 p.m.)* is a government-run *turicentro* one kilometre northwest of San Miguel off the Carretera Panamericana. It has swimming pools, lockers, gardens, restaurants and spots facilities, all set on spacious wooded grounds.

Complejo Turístico Limeño *($1.20; open every day 9 a.m. to 9 p.m.)* is a privately-run recreational centre one kilometre west of Santa Rosa de Lima along the Carretera Panamericana and then one kilometre south along a paved road in Cantón La Chorrera. It provides two swimming pools, a basketball court, restaurant and dance floor.

■ Beaches

Playa El Cuco ★ is situated 39 km (24 mi) south of San Miguel along a winding mountain road. Like most other beaches in El Salvador, this one has dark volcanic sand. It is very smooth and extends over many kilometres. Motorists occasionally go racing along the beach in their cars, and this can be quite disconcerting for sunbathers who are lying in the sand. The town of El Cuco has a number of very simple restaurants and some simple lodgings. More comfortable lodgings are also available, some of them several kilometres east along the beach. This is a popular weekend spot for people from San Miguel.

What we refer to here as the **Eastern Beaches** ★★ (there is no official name) extend along the southeastern tip of the Salvadoran coast near the westernmost entrance to the Gulf of Fonseca. **Playa El Tamarindo** ★ is the most easterly and actually faces the Gulf of Fonseca. It lies 23 km (14 mi) southwest of La Unión during high tide when a simple ferry operates across the shallow estuary that forms part of the route. Otherwise, the trip is about 15 km (9 mi) longer by a more roundabout route. The most westerly of these beaches is **Playa Las Tunas** ★. In between are six or eight other beaches, depending on how they are counted and what is considered a separate beach. The most important are **Playa El Jaguey** ★ and **Playa Negra** ★. A smaller beach called **Playa Torola** ★★ lies just east of Playa Las Tunas in a small, partly sheltered bay and, for practical purposes, is the private preserve of the Hotel Torola Cabaña Club, the most comfortable hotel in the region. The next most comfortable hotel is at Playa Negra, and a new hotel was under construction at Playa El Jaguey. Tourism, however, has yet to have much impact on this region.

All these beaches have volcanic sand, some of them darker than others. A couple of the smaller beaches are quite rocky. They are connected by a road running parallel to (and south of) the Carretera del Litoral. Bus 383 runs from La Unión, and bus 385 (less frequently) from San Miguel.

At Playa El Tamarindo there is a simple village whose inhabitants live largely from fishing. Visitors who care to rough it can inquire about huts where hammocks can be hung for a couple of dollars a night. There are also some very rudimentary eating places. The area is flat and shallow, and at high tide much of the beach disappears. The sand is quite dark. Bathers must go out a considerable distance before they are in deep water. In clear weather it is possible to peer across the Gulf of Fonseca from the beach and to view hilly territory in El Salvador, Honduras and Nicaragua simultaneously. (Honduras has only a very short coastline along the Gulf of Fonseca and a much longer coastline on the Caribbean side.)

In contrast to the very calm waters at Playa El Tamarindo, the other beaches face the open sea, and there is always the risk of getting caught in an undertow. The surf is not as strong, however, as it is further west. There are no lifeguards.

Another beach, **Playa El Icacal** ★, lies further west and can be reached via the town Intipucá, six kilometres (4 mi) north. It has strong surf and small stretches of sandy beach between rocky points.

Outdoor Activities

Hiking

Chaparrastique volcano, also known as the San Miguel volcano, is situated southwest of the city of the same name. The last big eruption was in 1976, when the night sky was illuminated with flames shooting from the cone. Since then there have been several minor eruptions that threw up smoke and ash. It takes about 3½ hours to climb, but most of this can be done by four-wheel-drive vehicle, with only the last hour or so by foot. The descent is considerably faster. From the ring of the cone, 2,130 m (5,981 ft) above sea level, it is possible to descend a series of steps about 200 m (656 ft) inside the volcano, where there is an expanse of sand almost like a beach. Stones thrown deeper into the volcano can release billows of sulphurous steam. It is difficult to find the way up to the volcano without a guide. Tereso de Jesús Ventura, a taxi driver and tour guide who speaks some English, can arrange visits (☎ 661-4210 in San Miguel and leave a message with Mario Cruz).

Conchagua volcano, south of La Unión, is another challenging climb. A starting point for the climb is the village of Amapalita, east of the town of Conchagua but more easily reached by a road running five kilometres (3 mi) south (and uphill) from the railway station in La Unión (the station is now used only for freight). Although the summit of the volcano lies only 1,243 m (4,078 ft) above sea level, it can be a slow climb because of heavy vegetation. There are spectacular views across the Gulf of Fonseca and into Honduras and Nicaragua.

Bicycling

Some of the secondary roads to the west of San Miguel can be interesting for cycling, including the roads through San Jorge, Chinameca or Santiago de María. This is hilly countryside with superb views, and you have to be in good shape to undertake it. The road to Berlín has some steep inclines. The countryside east of San Miguel is generally flat and uninteresting. The road to Perquín passes through scenic but very isolated areas, and the last few kilometres are unpaved.

Accommodation

■ San Miguel

All of the more comfortable hotels in San Miguel are located along the Carretera Panamericana, known also as

Avenida Roosevelt within the city limits. Rooms are generally set far enough from the highway so that noise is not a problem. There are a number of hotels in the city centre, but most are quite dismal.

Hotel del Centro *($13 ⊗, $21 ≡; tv; 8ª Calle Oriente, corner of 8ªAvenida Norte, ☎ 661-6913 or 661-5473)* is perhaps the least dismal of the city-centre hotels. Located 1½ blocks from the bus terminal, it has 31 small, simple, brightly furnished rooms set around a parking area.

Hotel China House *($15; ≡, ℜ, Carretera Panamericana on the western approach to the city)* has 20 small, quiet, dimly lit rooms which obviously have seen better days. There is a well lit sitting area beneath a shelter in the parking court. The restaurant serves Chinese and Salvadoran fare.

Hotel Milián *($13 per person; ≡, ≈, ℜ, Carretera Panamericana, across from the Hospital Militar, on the western approach to the city, ☎ 661-1242 or 661-1986)* has 35 brightly furnished motel-style rooms. It has an inexpensive open-air restaurant facing a noisy highway.

Hotel El Mandarín *($32, VI - MC - AE; ≡, tv, ≈, ℜ; Avenida Roosevelt 407, ☎ 661-6910)* is a sparkling new motel-style establishment with 22 pleasant rooms and a small pool at the edge of a big parking area. The restaurant has some Chinese dishes, but the Salvadoran dishes are better.

Trópico Inn *($41, VI - MC - AE - DC; ≡, ≈, ℜ, tv, bar; Avenida Roosevelt Sur 313, ☎ 661-0774)* is San Miguel's biggest and most lavish hotel. Its 100 rooms are large, with modern furniture and tile floors (a few have carpeting). It has both an indoor dining room with air conditioning and a more appealing outdoor dining area beneath a high thatched roof.

■ **Usulután**

Hotel España *($9, VI - MC; Calle Federico Penada 3, facing the Parque Central, ☎ 663-0378)* is a very traditional family-run hotel with 15 rooms set around a garden courtyard full of old furniture and knickknacks. Its old-fashioned rooms are big and clean, with fans and high ceilings, although a few are run-down. Both the low-slung, colonial-style building and the furnishings belong to other eras. What may be missing in comfort is made up for in charm.

Nevada Motor Inn *($12; ≡, tv; along the highway on the eastern edge of Usulután, near the bus terminal; ☎ 662-0206)* has small rooms with tacky modern furnishings and hidden garages for customers who take rooms by the hour. The hotel, however, is convenient to the bus terminal.

Hotel Las Palmeras *($17, ≡; two kilometres east of Usulután, then 50 metres north from the highway along a side road; ☎ 662-0161)* is easy to find thanks to signs that are clearly visible from the highway just east of Usulután. Its 45 motel-style rooms are small, bright, quiet and simply furnished.

■ **Playa El Cuco**

Prices in El Cuco often cover just a 12-hour period. Travellers who want a room for both the day and the night must sometimes pay twice! When a price is quoted, it is important to be sure what period is covered. Prices shown here cover 24 hours unless otherwise specified.

Several hotels are situated along the beach just east of the town of El Cuco and can be reached along a dirt road running parallel to the beach. Some, including **Hotel Cocolato** and **Motel Palmera**, are very run-down and cannot be recommended. A very inexpensive option is available near the town along the beach, where some simple huts with hammocks can be rented.

Hotel Leones Marinos *($17; near the beach on the eastern edge of town, ☎ 661-6366, extension 214)* is just a short distance from the sea. Its 18 fan-cooled rooms are small, bright and rather bare. They have both beds and hammocks but lack toilet seats. Some roms face a tree-shaded yard, while others have small terraces in front with hammocks.

Hospedaje La Tortuga *($15-$21; ₵ along the beach six kilometres east of El Cuco, no phone)* is for the self-sufficient. It consists of six bungalows set on broad palm-shaded grounds, some accommodating up to six persons. Rooms are small and bare, with whitewashed walls. Bedrooms are separate from the kitchen and bathroom, but interior walls do not reach the ceiling. Travellers must bring their own food and even their own bedsheets and pillows!

Tropiclub *($38 for 24 hours, $25 overnight only, $19 for day use, VI - MC - AE - DC; ≈, ℜ, bar; along the beach three kilometres east of El Cuco, ☎ 661-6366, extension 205, or contact the Trópico Inn in San Miguel, ☎ 661-0774)* has 12 four-bed cabins with thatched roofs and simple but attractive furnishings, plus hammocks and fans. Three larger air conditioned suites are also offered ($63 for 24 hours, $51 overnight, $38 day use).

The hotel is set on pleasant palm-shaded grounds facing the beach.

■ **Playa Torola**

Hotel Torola Cabaña Club *($69-$83, AE - DC; ≡, ≈, ℜ, bar; Playa Torola, next to Playa Las Tunas; ☎ 664-4516; in San Salvador, 224-0402 or 224-0403)* has a splendid setting on what amounts to a private beach, with low cliffs at either end. The beach is sandy in some places, rocky in others, and quite striking in appearance. Facing it is the pool, set beneath a rocky ledge. The hotel also plans to construct a salt-water pool below. The 24 rooms, some accommodating up to four people, are large and decently furnished. Rooms in the upper section of the hotel near the entrance are less interesting than those further down, facing the beach and the pool. The restaurant, with fish, seafood and meat dishes at reasonable prices, overlooks the beach (see p 135). There is also a large room that is sometimes used as a discotheque.

■ **Playa Negra**

Hotel Playa Negra *($35; ≡, ≈, ℜ; Playa Negra, ☎ 661-1726 or 661-1274, ⇄ 661-2513)* is set on pleasant, well shaded grounds next to the beach. Its 10 rooms are big, with tile floors, but are somewhat sparsely furnished. Some larger rooms ($46) can accommodate up to six people.

■ **La Unión**

Hotel Porto Bello *($5 ⊗, $11 ≡; 4ª Avenida Norte, corner of 1ª Calle Poniente, ☎ 664-4113)* is a city-centre hotel with 20 big, rather bare rooms, each with a bed and hammock. Rooms are set around a parking area. The hotel opened in 1994 but does not really look new. It is more appealing, however, than the other city-centre hotels.

Hotel y Restaurant Pelícano *($7 single ⊗, $15 single or double ≡, tv, $26 with two double beds; six kilometres west of La Unión along the Carretera Panamericana to Cantón El Guisquil, then one kilometre north along a side road, ☏ 664-4649)* is set at the edge of a tidal plain, where many birds flock at low tide. There is fishing nearby. Rooms are simple and comfortably furnished, facing the tidal plain on one side and a large, barren paved area on the other. Lying at the far end, the restaurant (see p 136) is good but does not open early for breakfast. The hotel can be reached from La Unión by local bus 54.

■ Santa Rosa de Lima

Hotel Florida *($3 per person; in the city centre, opposite the Banco del Desarrollo, ☏ 664-2020)* is set in a colonial-style building with lots of plants and has 16 small, dark, very simply furnished rooms with shared bath.

Hospedaje El Salvador *($4 single, $6 double; Calle Antigua Ruta Militar, near 4ª Avenida Norte, ☏ 664-2230)* is situated a short way east of the city centre on an unpaved street near the Esso station. Its 18 rooms are clean and simple, each with a bed, hammock, fan, table and chair, but bathrooms are shared. The hotel is set in a colonial-style building with a paved-over courtyard.

Hotel El Recreo *($5 per person; in the city centre, opposite the Antel building, one block from the church and the market, ☏ 664-2126)* is often suggested to visitors, but really it should not be. Rooms are dark and poorly furnished, and the place is not kept very clean. Although there are private bathrooms, the water supply is unreliable.

■ San Francisco Gotera

Hotel Unicornio y Liz Café *($12, tv, ℜ; Avenida Thompson Norte, corner of Calle Simeón Cañas, ☏ 664-0118)* has 12 rooms that are clean, quiet and reasonably furnished, but bathrooms are shared. Rooms face a tree-shaded concrete courtyard.

■ Perquín

For visitors who decide to stay here overnight, the pickings are rather slim. The dark and dreary **Casa de Huéspedes El Gigante** charges $3 per person in four-bed dormitories, which means that a private room costs $12, without private bath. It is situated on a side road below the cemetery near the entrance to the town. There are no phones.

✕ Restaurants

As is the case virtually everywhere outside San Salvador, dining is casual and reservations are practically an unknown phenomenon. For quick meals, fried chicken is easy to find in all the larger towns, and pizza or hamburgers are found in a few spots. *Pupusas*, cornmeal tortillas stuffed with beans, cheese or other fillings, are excellent for snacks or light meals and have saved many a vegetarian from starvation.

The greatest culinary delight in eastern El Salvador, found only in a handful of places, is a seafood soup or stew called a *mariscada*, containing lobster, crab, shrimp, fish and other ingredients cooked in a special broth. Each restaurant that offers it has developed its own secret recipe. Three are mentioned toward the bottom of the list below.

■ San Miguel

La Pampa Argentina *(main courses $6-$10, 12 p.m. to 2:30 p.m. and 6 pm. to 10:30 p.m; Avenida Roosevelt across from the Trópico Inn)* is thatch-roofed, fan-cooled and pleasant. The specialty is beef. A big Argentine-style *churrasco* (steak) or mixed grill costs $8. Shrimp is also offered. Seafood cocktails and *ceviches* (cocktails of marinated fish or shrimp) make good appetizers ($3).

Baty Carnitas *(main courses $6-$11; 8 a.m. to 9 p.m., closed Sunday; 4ª Calle Poniente 108, next to Pollo Campero)* has a casual atmosphere with an air-conditioned dining room and a small terrace in front. The house specialties are a mixed grill of meat and shrimp, $15 for two people, and the grilled seafood platter, $11 for one.

El Gran Tejano *(main courses $6-$9; 12 p.m. to 9 p.m.; 4ª Calle Oriente 108, next to Banco Salvadoreño del Centro)* has a U.S. cowboy motif, with air conditioning and tablecloths. Steak dominates the menu, with some shrimp dishes.

Los Ranchos *(main courses $7-$8; 10 a.m. to 9 p.m.; just north of San Miguel on the highway to San Francisco Gotera)* is an open-air garden restaurant with a series of thatched shelters and a variety of steak and shrimp dishes. The wooden stools are nice to look at but not to sit on.

■ Usulután

Lathio's *(main courses $5-$9; facing the Parque Central)* offers a variety of meat and seafood dishes. Part of the dining room overlooks the park.

■ Eastern Beaches

Hotel Torola Cabaña Club *(main courses $5-$11; Playa Torola, next to Playa Las Tunas)* has a restaurant that is noteworthy for its views of a dramatic, cliff-bordered beach. The menu has a variety of fish, seafood and meat dishes, including a special *mariscada* (mixed seafood stew) for $8.

Ranchón Brisas del Pacífico *(main courses $3-$5; Playa El Jaguey)* has a big thatched shelter and red tablecloths. It is along the road, away from the beach. It offers shrimp and mixed seafood dishes, as well as beef and chicken.

■ La Unión

Miramar *(main courses $5-$6; 10 a.m. to 8 p.m.; Punta de la Rábida, by the water's edge)* is an open-air restaurant with a peaceful seaside setting by the edge of a quiet inlet, near the city centre. Shrimp, fish and lobster dishes are surprisingly cheap.

Right next door and similar, is **Amanecer Marino**, but for some bizarre and unfortunate reason a parking area was built between the restaurant and the water's edge.

Los Gallos *(main courses $4-$6; 3ª Avenida Sur at 4ª Calle Oriente, near the railway station)* is an open-air restaurant with a thatched roof, wooden chairs and tables, and a Mexican menu featuring tacos, shrimp and beef.

El Pelícano *(main courses $3-$6; 9 a.m. to 9 p.m.; six kilometres west of La Unión along the Carretera Panamericana to Cantón El Guisquil, then one kilometre north along a side road, local bus 54)* is an open-air restaurant set at the edge of a tidal plain. There are many fish, shrimp and meat dishes on the menu. The house specialty is the *Cazuela Pelícano* ($6), a *mariscada*, or seafood stew, containing lobster, crab, shrimp, oyster and fish.

■ Santa Rosa de Lima

La Pema *(main course $7; Tue to Sun, 10 a.m. to 4 p.m.; in the centre of town next to the Banco de Comercio)* may be the best known restaurant in eastern El Salvador. The owner has built her fame around her *mariscada*, a seafood stew containing lobster, crab, greyfish and shrimp cooked in a secret broth and served with hot cheese-stuffed tortillas. She also offers grilled meats, but nearly everyone asks for the *mariscada*. The restaurant is set around a large courtyard with a wooden ceiling and red tablecloths.

Entertainment

On the outskirts of San Miguel, across from the China House hotel, is a somewhat seedy night club called **Tony's**, with live bands most evenings. Unfortunately, that's about as exciting as it seems to get. Elsewhere, the possibilities for evening entertainment are even more limited.

Shopping

San Miguel has two big, glittery new shopping centres, including an imitation of San Salvador's Metrocentro that was nearing completion in 1994. The merchandise, by and large, is what you might find almost anywhere. At the market in Santa Rosa de Lima, there are some interesting hammocks and blankets, as well as a few items from Honduras. For the most part, however, travellers seeking original handicrafts are likely to be disappointed in eastern El Salvador. Little is produced in this part of the country, although a handful of shops offer items from elsewhere.

GLOSSARY

GREETINGS

Goodbye	*adiós, hasta luego*
Good afternoon and good evening	*buenas tardes*
Hi (casual)	*hola*
Hello (during the day)	*buenos días*
Good night	*buenas noches*
Thank-you	*gracias*
Please	*por favor*
You are welcome	*de nada*
Excuse-me	*perdone/a*
My family name is...	*mi apellido es...*
My first name is...	*mi nombre es...*
yes	*no*
no	*sí*
Do you speak English?	*¿habla usted inglés?*
Slower, please	*más despacio, por favor*
What is you name?	*¿cómo se llama usted?*
How are you?	*¿qué tal?*
I am fine	*estoy bien*
single (m/f)	*soltero/a*
divorced (m/f)	*divorciado/a*
married (m/f)	*casado a*
friend (m/f)	*amigo/a*
child (m/f)	*niño/a*
husband, wife	*esposo/a*
mother	*madre*
father	*padre*
brother, sister	*hermano/a*
widower widow	*viudo/a*
I am Canadian	*Soy canadiense*
I am American (male/female)	*Soy americano/a*
I am Belgian	*Soy belga*
I am Swiss	*Soy suizo*
I am British (male/female)	*Soy britanico/a*
I am Italian (male/female)	*Soy italiano/a*
I am German (male/female)	*Soy alemán/a*
I am a tourist	*Soy turista*
I am sorry, I don't speak Spanish	*Lo siento, no hablo español*

138 Glossary

DIRECTIONS

beside	*al lado de*
to the right	*a la derecha*
to the left	*a la izquierda*
into, inside	*dentro*
behind	*detrás*
in front of	*delante*
outside	*fuera*
enter	*entre*
here	*aquí*
there	*allí*
far from	*lejos de*
Where is ... ?	*¿dónde está ... ?*
To get to ...?	*¿para ir a...?*
near	*cerca de*
straight ahead	*todo recto*
Is there a tourism office here?	*¿hay aquí una oficina de turismo?*

MONEY

money	*dinero / plata*
credit card	*tarjeta de crédito*
exchange	*cambio*
traveller's cheque	*cheque de viaje*
I don't have any money	*no tengo dinero*
The bill, please	*la cuenta, por favor*
receipt	*recibo*

SHOPPING

a department store	*almacén*
a store	*una tienda*
closed	*cerrado/a*
open	*abierto/a*
How much is this?	*¿cuánto es?*
I need...	*me necesita ...*
the customer	*el / la cliente*
the market	*mercado*
to buy	*comprar*
to sell	*vender*
salesperson	*dependiente*
salesperson (male/female)	*vendedor/a*
I would like...	*quería...*
batteries	*pilas*
blouse	*la blusa*
cameras	*cámaras*

Glossary

cosmetics and perfumes	*cosméticos y perfumes*
cotton	*algodón*
eyeglasses	*las gafas*
fabric	*tela*
gifts	*regalos*
gold	*oro*
handbag	*una bolsa*
hat	*el sombrero*
jacket	*la chaqueta*
jeans	*los tejanos*
jewellery	*joyeros*
leather	*cuero / piel*
local crafts	*artesanía típica*
magazines	*revistas*
newpapers	*periódicos*
pants	*los pantalones*
photographic film	*película*
precious stones	*piedras preciosas*
records, cassettes	*discos, cassettes*
sandals	*las sandalias*
shirt	*la camisa*
shoes	*los zapatos*
silver	*plata*
skirt	*la falda*
sun screen products	*productos solares*
T-shirt	*la camiseta*
watches	*relojes*
wool	*lana*

MISCELLANEOUS

a little	*poco*
a lot	*mucho*
bad	*malo*
beautiful	*hermoso*
big	*grande*
big, tall (person)	*grande*
cold	*frío*
dark	*oscuro*
do not touch	*no tocar*
expensive	*caro*
fat	*gordo*
good	*bueno*
hot	*caliente*
I am hungry	*tengo hambre*
I am ill	*estoy enfermo (enferma)*
I am thirsty	*tengo sed*

140 Glossary

less	*menos*
light (colour)	*claro*
more	*más*
narrow	*estrecho*
new	*nuevo*
not expensive	*barato*
nothing	*nada*
old	*viejo*
pretty	*bonito*
quickly	*rápidamente*
short (length)	*corto*
short (person)	*bajo*
slim, skinny	*delgado*
slowly	*despacio*
small	*pequeño*
something	*algo*
ugly	*feo*
What is this?	*¿qué es esto?*
when?	*¿cuando?*
where?	*¿dónde?*
wide	*ancho*

NUMBERS

1	*uno ou una*		23	*veintitrés*
2	*dos*		24	*veinticuatro*
3	*tres*		25	*veinticinco*
4	*cuatro*		26	*veintiséis*
5	*cinco*		27	*veintisiete*
6	*seis*		28	*veintiocho*
7	*siete*		29	*veintinueve*
8	*ocho*		30	*treinta*
9	*nueve*		31	*treinta y uno*
10	*diez*		32	*treinta y dos*
11	*once*		40	*cuarenta*
12	*doce*		50	*cincuenta*
13	*trece*		60	*sesenta*
14	*catorce*		70	*setenta*
15	*quince*		80	*ochenta*
16	*dieciséis*		90	*noventa*
17	*diecisiete*		100	*cien* or *ciento*
18	*dieciocho*		200	*doscientos, doscientas*
19	*diecinueve*		500	*quinientos, quinientas*
20	*veinte*		1,000	*mil*
21	*veintiuno*		10,000	*diez mil*
22	*veintidós*		1,000,000	*un millón*

WEATHER

clouds	*nubes*
It is cold out.	*hace frío*
It is hot out.	*hace calor*
rain	*lluvia*
sun	*sol*

TIME

afternoon, evening	*tarde*
day	*día*
ever	*jamás*
hour	*hora*
in the morning	*por la mañana*
minute	*minuto*
month	*mes*
never	*nunca*
night	*noche*
now	*ahora*
today	*hoy*
tommorrow	*mañana*
week	*semana*
What time is it?	*¿qué hora es?*
year	*año*
yesterday	*ayer*
Sunday	*domingo*
Monday	*lunes*
Tuesday	*martes*
Wednesday	*miércoles*
Thursday	*jueves*
Friday	*viernes*
Saturday	*sábado*
January	*enero*
February	*febrero*
March	*marzo*
April	*abril*
May	*mayo*
June	*junio*
July	*julio*
August	*agosto*
September	*septiembre*
October	*octubre*
November	*noviembre*
December	*diciembre*

COMMUNICATION

air mail	*correos aéreo*
collect call	*llamada por cobrar*
dial the regional code	*marcar el prefijo*
envelope	*sobre*
fax	*telefax*
long distance	*larga distancia*
post and telegram office	*correos y telégrafos*
post office	*la oficina de correos*
rate	*tarifa*
stamps	*sellos*
telegram	*telegrama*
telephone book	*un listín de teléfonos*
wait for the tone	*esperar la señal*

ACTIVITIES

beach	*playa*
museum or gallery	*museo*
scuba diving	*buceo*
to swim	*bañarse*
to walk around	*pasear*

TRANSPORTATION

airport	*aeropuerto*
arrival	*llegada*
avenue	*avenida*
bagage	*equipajes*
bicycle	*la bicicleta*
boat	*el buque*
bus	*el bus*
bus stop	*una parada de autobús*
cancelled	*annular*
car	*la coche, el carro*
collective taxi	*colectivo*
corner	*esquina*
departure	*salida*
east	*este*
fast	*rápido*
neighbourhood	*barrio*
north	*norte*
on time	*a la hora*
one way ticket	*ida*
plane	*el avión*
return	*regreso*
return ticket	*ida y vuelta*

Glossary 143

schedule	*horario*
south	*sur*
station	*estación*
street	*calle*
sure, safe	*seguro*
The bus stop, please	*la parada, por favor*
train	*el tren*
train crossing	*crucero ferrocarril*
west	*oeste*

CARS

can be rented, takes passengers	*alquilar*
danger, be careful	*cuidado*
gas	*petróleo, gasolina*
highway	*autopista*
no parking	*prohibido aparcar*
no passing	*no adelantar*
parking	*parqueo*
pedestrians	*peatones*
road closed, no through traffic	*no hay paso*
service station	*servicentro*
slow down	*reduzca velocidad*
speed limit	*velocidad permitida*
stop	*alto*
stop! (an order)	*pare*
traffic light	*semáforo*

ACCOMMODATION

(beach) cabin, bungalow	*cabaña*
accommodation	*alojamiento*
air conditioning	*aire condicionado*
bathroom	*baños*
bed	*cama*
breakfast	*desayuno*
double, for two people	*doble*
elevator	*ascensor*
fan	*ventilador*
floor (first, second...)	*piso*
high/off season	*temporada alta/baja*
hot water	*agua caliente*
main floor	*planta baja*
manager, boss	*gerente, jefe*
pool	*piscina*
room	*habitación*
single, for one person	*sencillo*
with bathroom	*con baño*

INDEX

Acajutla (Western El Salvador) . . 105
    Accommodation 114
    Restaurants 116
Accommodation, General
        Information 44
Agua Fría (Central El Salvador)
    Parks 90
Ahuachapán (Western El
        Salvador) 107
    Accommodation 114
    Restaurants 116
    Shopping 117
Air Travel, Taxes 42
Airline Offices (San Salvador) . . . 61
Airplanes, Domestic 39
Airports (San Salvador) 60
Alcohol, Customs 24
Altos de la Cueva (Eastern El
        Salvador) 130
Amapulapa Turicentro (Central El
        Salvador) 89
Apaneca (Western El Salvador) . . 107
    Accommodation 114
    Restaurants 116
Apastepeque (Central El
        Salvador)
    Parks 90
Apulo Turicentro (San Salvador) . 67
Art Galleries (San Salvador) 78
Arts and Leisure 21
Atecozol Turicentro (Western El
        Salvador) 111
Bacterial Disorders 32
Barra de Santiago (Western El
        Salvador) 105
    Beaches 111
    Swimming 112
Bars (San Salvador) 77
Basílica de la Ceiba de Guadalupe
        (San Salvador) 64
Beach Safety 35
Beaches
    Eastern El Salvador 130
    General Information 51
    San Salvador 67
    Western El Salvador 111

Berlín (Eastern El Salvador) . . . 124
Bicycling
    Central El Salvador 93
    Eastern El Salvador 131
    General Information 52
    Western El Salvador 112
Boating
    Central El Salvador 93
    General Information 52
    Western El Salvador 111
Bus Schedules 38
Bus Terminals 38
Buses 37
Business Hours and Holidays . . . 49
Camping 44
    Cerro Verde 113
Capilla de la Divina Providencia
        (San Salvador) 66
Car Rental 35
Car Rentals 59
Carretera Panamericana 100
Cars 35
Cars, Customs 25
Casa Presidencial (San Salvador) 66
Casco de la Hacienda (Western El
        Salvador) 110
Catedral Metropolitana (San
        Salvador) 62
Cathedral (San Miguel) 123
Cathedral (San Vicente) 89
Cathedral (Santa Ana) 104
Cathedral (Sonsonate) 105
Cementerio General (San Miguel) 123
Central El Salvador 81
    Accommodation 93
    By Bus 83
    By Car 82
    By Taxi 84
    Entertainment 96
    Exploring 84
    Finding Your Way Around . . 82
    Outdoor Activities 92
    Parks and Beaches 89
    Restaurants 95
    Shopping 97
Cerro El Pital (La Palma)
    Hiking 92

Index

Cerro Verde (Western El
    Salvador) 104
    Accommodation 113
    Restaurants 115
Cerro Verde, Parque Nacional ... 109
    Hiking 111
Chalatenango (Central El
    Salvador) 86
    Restaurants 96
Chalchuapa (Western El
    Salvador) 107
    Accommodation 115
    Shopping 117
Chaparrastique Volcano (Eastern
    El Salvador) 131
Chinameca (Eastern El Salvador) . 123
Church (Perquín) 128
Cinema (San Salvador) 76
Civil War 15
Climate 33
Clinics 33
Clock Tower (San Vicente) 89
Cojutepeque (Central El Salvador) 88
    Shopping 97
Colonia Escalón (San Salvador) .. 64
    Accommodation 71
    Restaurants 74
Colonia La Mascota (San
    Salvador)
    Restaurants 74
Complejo Turístico Limeño
    (Eastern El Salvador) .. 130
Conchagua (Eastern El Salvador) . 127
Conchagua Volcano (Eastern El
    Salvador) 131
Costa del Bálsamo (Western El
    Salvador) 106
Costa Del Sol (Central El
    Salvador)
    Accommodation 94
    Beaches 90
    Parks 90
    Restaurants 96
Credit Cards 41
Cuisine 46
Cuisnahuat (Western El Salvador) 106
Culture and Society 20
Customs 24
Cutuco (La Unión) 126

Diarrhea 32
Eastern Beaches (Eastern El
    Salvador) 130
    Restaurants 135
Eastern El Salvador 119
    Accommodation 131
    By Air 122
    By Bus 121
    By Car 120
    By Taxi 122
    Entertainment 136
    Exploring 123
    Finding Your Way Around . 120
    Outdoor Activities 131
    Parks and Beaches 129
    Restaurants 134
    Shopping 136
Economy 19
El Mozote (Eastern El Salvador) 129
El Salvador del Mundo (San
    Salvador) 64
El Salvador in Statistics 22
El Tazumal, Ruins of (Western El
    Salvador) 107
El Trifinio 110
Electricity 49
Embassies and Consulates 25
Embassies and Consulates (El
    Salvador) Abroad 26
Embassies and Consulates
    (Foreign) in San
    Salvador 25
Entering the Country 29
    By Air 29
    By Bus 30
    By Car 30
    By Rail or Sea 31
Entertainment, General
    Information 46
Entrance Formalities 23
Estadio Cuscatlán (San Salvador) 64
Estadio Nacional (San Salvador) . 64
Estero de Jaltepeque (Central El
    Salvador) 90
    Swimming and Boating 93
Exchange Rates 40
Exchanging Money 39
Exports, Customs 25
Fauna 12

Index

Fax 43
Feria Internacional de El Salvador
    (San Salvador) 64
Firearms, Customs 25
Fishermen's El Salvador (La
    Libertad) 92
Flora and Fauna 12
Fruits, Customs 24
Fútbol 47
    San Salvador 76
Geography 10
Glossary 137
    Accommodation 143
    Activities 142
    Cars 143
    Communication 142
    Directions 138
    Greetings 137
    Miscellaneous 139
    Money 138
    Numbers 140
    Shopping 138
    Time 141
    Transportation 142
    Weather 141
Golf, General Information 53
Gran Mirador de los Planes
    (Panchimalco) 67
Guazapa (Central El Salvador)
    Hiking 93
Handicrafts (San Salvador) 78
Health 31
Highways 35
Hiking
    Central El Salvador 92
    Cerro Verde (Western El
        Salvador) 111
    Eastern El Salvador 131
    General Information 52
    Reserva Natural de
        Montecristo (Western El
        Salvador) 111
    San Salvador 68
    Western El Salvador 111
History 13
Hitchhiking 39
Holidays 49
Hospedajes 44

Hotel Malecón De Don Lito (La
    Libertad) 92
Hotels 44
Ichanmichen Turicentro (Central
    El Salvador) 89
Iglesia Asunción (Izalco) 105
Iglesia Dolores (Izalco) 105
Iglesia El Calvario (Santa Ana) . 104
Iglesia El Carmen (Santa Ana) .. 104
Iglesia El Pilar (San Vicente) 89
Iglesia El Rosario (San Salvador) . 62
Iglesia La Parroquia (Metapán) . 108
Iglesia Medalla Milagrosa (San
    Miguel) 123
Iglesia Nuestra Señora del Pilar
    (Sonsonate) 105
Iglesia Parroquial (Sonsonate) .. 105
Ilobasco (Central El Salvador) ... 88
    Shopping 97
Income 20
Insurance 31
Isla Conchaguita (Eastern El
    Salvador) 126
Isla Meanguera (Eastern El
    Salvador) 126
Isla Zacatillo (Eastern El
    Salvador) 126
Islands of Gulf of Fonseca
    (Eastern El Salvador) . 126
Izalco (Western El Salvador) ... 105
Joya de Cerén (Central El
    Salvador) 84
Juayúa (Western El Salvador) .. 107
    Accommodation 114
    Restaurants 116
La Libertad (Central El Salvador)
    Accommodation 94
    Beaches 91
    Restaurants 96
La Palma (Central El Salvador) .. 86
    Accommodation 93
    Hiking 92
    Restaurants 96
    Shopping 97
La Unión (Eastern El Salvador) . 126
    Accommodation 133
    Restaurants 135

Index

Lago de Coatepeque (Western El
    Salvador) 104
    Accommodation 112
    Restaurants 115
    Swimming and Boating 111
Lago de Güija (Western El
    Salvador) 108
    Swimming and Boating 111
Lago de Ilopango (San Salvador)
    Accommodation 72
Lagode Ilopango (San Salvador) . 67
Laguna de Alegría (Berlín) 124
Laguna de Apastepeque (Central
    El Salvador) 89
    Swimming and Boating 93
Laguna de Jocotal (Eastern El
    Salvador) 129
Laguna Verde (Western El
    Salvador) 107
    Hiking 111
Language 42
Leather, Customs 24
Long-Distance Telephones (San
    Salvador) 61
Los Ausoles (Ahuachapán) 107
Los Ausoles de la Viejona
    (Chinameca) 124
Los Chorros Turicentro 67
Los Planes de Montecristo 110
Los Tecomates (La Palma)
    Hiking 92
Mail 43
Mail and Telecommunications ... 43
Mercado Central (San Salvador) . 62
Mercado Ex-Cuartel (San
    Salvador) 62, 78
Mercado Nacional de Artesanías
    (San Salvador) 64, 78
Metapán (Western El Salvador) . . 108
    Accommodation 115
Metrocentro (San Salvador) 78
Metrosur (San Salvador) 78
Miramundo (La Palma)
    Hiking 92
Miscellaneous Practical
    Information 48
Money and Banking 39

Montecristo,
    Reserva Natural de ... 108, 109
    Hiking 111
Monumento a la Revolución (San
    Salvador) 64
Museo de la Revolución
    Salvadoreña (Perquín) . 128
Museo Nacional David Guzmán
    (San Salvador) 64
Nahuizalco (Western El Salvador) 106
    Shopping 117
Nature Reserves, General
    Information 52
Outdoor Activities 51
    Beaches and Swimming ... 51
    Bicycling 52
    Boating 52
    Hiking 52
    Nature Reserves 52
    Surfing 52
    Tennis and Golf 53
Ozatlán (Eastern El Salvador) . . 124
Packing 33
Palacio Municipal (Santa Ana) . 104
Palacio Nacional (San Salvador) . 62
Panchimalco 67
Parks
    Central El Salvador 89
    Eastern El Salvador 129
    San Salvador 67
    Western El Salvador 109
Parque Balboa (San Salvador) ... 67
Parque Central (Cojutepeque) ... 88
Parque Central (Ilobasco) 88
Parque Central (San Vicente) ... 89
Parque Central (Santa Ana) ... 104
Parque Cuscatlán (San Salvador) 64
Parque Zoológico Nacional (San
    Salvador) 66
Passports 23
Perquín (Eastern El Salvador) . . 127
    Accommodation 134
Pets, Customs 25
Pharmacies 33
Plants, Customs 24
Playa Conchalío (La Libertad) ... 92
Playa Costa Del Sol (Costa Del
    Sol) 90

Index

Playa de Metalío (Western El
  Salvador) 111
Playa El Cuco (Eastern El
  Salvador) 130
  Accommodation 132
Playa El Espino (Usulután) 126
Playa El Icacal (Eastern El
  Salvador) 131
Playa El Jaguey (Eastern El
  Salvador) 130
Playa El Majahual (La Libertad) .. 92
Playa El Sunzal (La Libertad) 92
Playa El Tamarindo (Eastern El
  Salvador) 130
Playa El Tunco (La Libertad) 92
Playa La Paz (La Libertad) 92
Playa Las Flores (La Libertad) ... 92
Playa Las Tunas (Eastern El
  Salvador) 130
Playa Los Blancos (Costa Del Sol) 90
Playa Los Cóbanos (Western El
  Salvador) 111
Playa Majahual (Isla Meanguera) . 126
Playa Negra (Eastern El Salvador) 130
  Accommodation 133
Playa San Blas (La Libertad) 92
Playa San Diego (La Libertad) ... 92
Playa San Marcelino (Costa Del
  Sol) 90
Playa Torola (Eastern El Salvador) 130
  Accommodation 133
Plaza Barrios (San Salvador) 62
Plaza Las Américas (San
  Salvador) 64
Plaza Libertad (San Salvador) ... 62
Plaza Morazán (San Salvador) ... 62
Politics 17
Portrait of El Salvador 9
  Arts and Leisure 21
  Economy 19
  Flora and Fauna 12
  Geography 10
  History 13
  Politics 17
  Society and Culture 20
Practical Information 23
  Accommodation 44
  Climate 33
  Customs 24
  Embassies and Consulates .. 25
  Entering the Country 29
  Entertainment 46
  Entrance Formalities 23
  Health 31
  Insurance 31
  Language 42
  Mail and
    Telecommunications ... 43
  Miscellaneous 48
  Money and Banking 39
  Packing 33
  Restaurants 45
  Safety and Security 34
  San Salvador 60
  Shopping 47
  The Press 48
  Tourist Information 28
  Transportation 35
Press 48
Pronunciation in Spanish 42
Puerta del Diablo (San Salvador) . 67
Race 20
Religion 20
Renting a Car 35
Reserva Natural de Montecristo 108,
                                        109, 111
Restaurants, General Information 45
Río Nunuapa (Central El
  Salvador)
    Hiking 92
    Swimming and Boating 93
Romero, Oscar Amulfo 66
Ruinas de San Andrés (Central El
  Salvador) 86
Safety and Security 34
  At the Beach 35
  Women Travellers 35
Saints' Days 47
Salcoatitán (Western El Salvador) 106
San Antonio del Monte (Western
  El Salvador) 105
San Francisco Gotera (Eastern El
  Salvador) 127
  Accommodation 134
San Jorge (Eastern El Salvador) 124
San Julián (Western El Salvador) 106
San Marcelino (Central El
  Salvador) 90

Index

San Miguel (Eastern El Salvador) . 123
    Accommodation 131
    Restaurants 135
San Salvador 55
    Accommodation 68
    Airline Offices 61
    Airports 60
    By Bus 58
    By Car 59
    By Foot 60
    By Taxi 59
    Entertainment 76
    Exploring 62
    Finding Your Way Around . . 57
    General Orientation 57
    Intercity Buses 58
    Long-Distance Telephone . . . 61
    Outdoor Activities 68
    Parks and Beaches 67
    Practical Information 60
    Restaurants 72
    Shopping 78
    Tourist Information 60
San Salvador - City Centre 62
San Salvador - West of the City
    Centre 64
San Salvador Volcano (Hiking) . . 68
San Sebastián (Central El
    Salvador) 88
San Vicente (Central El Salvador) 88
    Accommodation 94
    Restaurants 96
San Vicente Volcano (San
    Vicente) 89
Santa Ana (Western El Salvador) 102
    Accommodation 112
    Restaurants 115
Santa Rosa de Lima (Eastern El
    Salvador) 127
    Accommodation 134
    Restaurants 136
Santo Domingo de Guzmán
    (Western El Salvador) . . 106
Segunda Monte (Eastern El
    Salvador) 129
Sending Money 41
Shopping, General Information . . 47
Sihuatehuacán, Turicentro 111
Soccer 47

Society and Culture 20
Sonsonate (Area North and
    West) 106
Sonsonate (Western El Salvador) 105
    Accommodation 113
    Restaurants 116
    Shopping 117
Statistics 22
Sun 32
Surfing, General Information . . . 52
Swimming
    Central El Salvador 90, 93
    Eastern El Salvador 129
    General Information 51
    San Salvador 67
    Western El Salvador 111
Taxes and Tipping 41
Taxes on Air Travel 42
Taxis 37
Teatro Nacional (San Salvador) 62, 77
Teatro Nacional de Santa Ana
    (Santa Ana) 104
Telephone 43
Tennis, General Information 53
Theatre (San Salvador) 76
Time Zone 49
Tipping 42
Tobacco, Customs 24
Tourist Information 28
Tourist Information (San
    Salvador) 60
Tours, Organized 29
Trains 39
Transportation 35
Traveller's Cheques 40
Turicentro Altos de la Cueva
    (San Miguel) 123
Turicentro Atecozol (Izalco) . . . 105
Turicentro Sihuatehuacán (Santa
    Ana) 104
Turicentros 28
U.S. Embassy (San Salvador) . . . 66
Universidad Centroamericana
    (San Salvador) 64
Universidad Nacional de El
    Salvador (San Salvador) 64
Usulután (Eastern El Salvador) . 124
    Accommodation 132
    Restaurants 135

Vaccinations	31
Value-Added Tax	41
Vegetables, Customs	24
Virgen de Fátima (Cojutepeque)	88
Visas	23
Water and Alcohol	32
Weights and Measures	49
Western Coast	105
Western El Salvador	99
Accommodation	112
By Bus	101
By Car	100
By Rail	102
By Taxi	102
Entertainment	116
Exploring	102
Finding Your Way Around	100
Outdoor Activities	111
Parks and Beaches	109
Restaurants	115
Shopping	117
Women Travellers	35
Zacatecoluca (Central El Salvador)	89
Zona Rosa (Restaurants)	73

Travel Notes

◼ ULYSSES TRAVEL GUIDES

- ☐ Best Bed & Breakfasts in Québec $9.95
- ☐ Dominican Republic 2nd Edition $22.95
- ☐ Guadeloupe $22.95
- ☐ Martinique $22.95
- ☐ Montréal $22.95
- ☐ Ontario $14.95
- ☐ Panamá $22.95
- ☐ Québec $24.95
- ☐ El Salvador $22.95

◼ ULYSSES GREEN ESCAPES

- ☐ Hiking North-East USA $19.95
- ☐ Hiking Québec $19.95

◼ ULYSSES DUE SOUTH

- ☐ Cartagena $ 9.95
- ☐ Nicaragua $ 9.95
- ☐ Puerto Plata $ 9.95

◼ ULYSSES TRAVEL JOURNAL

- ☐ Ulysses Travel Journal $9.95

QUANTITY	TITLES	PRICE	TOTAL

Name : _____

Address : _____

City : _____

Postal Code : _____

Payment : ☐ Money Order ☐ Visa ☐ MC ☐ Cheque

Card Number : _____

Expiry Date : _____

Signature : _____

Sub-total	
Postage & Handling	3.00 $
Sub-total	
G.S.T. in Canada 7 %	
TOTAL	

ULYSSES TRAVEL PUBLICATIONS

4176, Saint-Denis
Montréal, Québec
H2W 2M5
Tel : (514) 843-9882
Fax: (514) 843-9448